VISIONS OF A WORLD HUNGRY

STUDY, PRAYER, & ACTION

VISIONS OF A WORLD HUNGRY

STUDY, PRAYER, & ACTION

Thomas G. Pettepiece

NASHVILLE, TENNESSEE

VISIONS OF A WORLD HUNGRY: STUDY, PRAYER, AND ACTION

The scripture quotations identified RSV are from the Revised Standard Version of the Bible, copyrighted 1946, 1952 and © 1971 by the Division of Christian Education, National Council of the Churches of Christ in the United States of America, and are used by permission.

Quotations from *The New English Bible*, © The Delegates of the Oxford University Press and Syndics of the Cambridge University Press 1961 and 1970, are reprinted by permission. The initials NEB are used to identify *New English Bible* quotations.

Quotations from the *Good News Bible, The Bible in Today's English Version* (TEV), copyright by American Bible Society 1966, 1971, © 1976, are used by permission.

Quotations from *Between a Rock and a Hard Place* by Mark Hatfield, published by Word Books, Publisher, Waco, Texas, and © 1976, are used by permission of the publisher.

Cover transparency by Tom Pettepiece

First printing, April, 1979(8)

Library of Congress Catalog Card Number: 79-63097

ISBN 0-8358-0371-6

Printed in the United States of America

For Chris and Brian
and their children's children

CONTENTS

VISIONS
OF A
WORLD
HUNGRY

STUDY, PRAYER, & ACTION

FOREWORD

I consider *Visions of a World Hungry* to be a very special book because it helps to fill a very special need. Both Old Testament and New Testament urge us in the strongest possible terms to show love and justice to hungry people. But the problem is so massive that we tend to be overwhelmed, incapable of responding with more than an occasional token contribution for world relief. This book helps us out of that dilemma. It helps us perceive hunger not simply through an abstract intellectual exercise, but in our prayers and in personal reflection out of which prayer emerges.

In doing this, author Tom Pettepiece performs another useful service. He helps break down the false separation we sometimes create by putting worship in one compartment and social justice in another—usually preferring one to the other, forgetting that both are central to Christian faith.

Not every reader will agree with every expression, every suggestion, or every emphasis in the book. However, because of the book's adaptability, each reader can readily add, subtract, or revise any part to make the book more useful for private or even corporate devotions. The chapters can be used for group discussion, as well.

I like this book for many reasons. One, it reflects the fact that hunger is a public policy issue. Further, it cor-rectly links hunger to a wide variety of related issues. What impresses me most about the book, however, is the sense of gratitude and joy that flows from it. In the long run, guilt immobilizes us, while the gospel sets us free to be people for others. Mr. Pettepiece knows this and in this book invites us to celebrate the Kingdom.

I have no doubt that members of Bread for the World will welcome this volume and use it as a valuable resource individually and in BFW gatherings across the land. And I hope that countless others will, through this fine book, discover the joy of celebrating the gospel and responding to hungry people.

—ARTHUR SIMON, EXECUTIVE DIRECTOR,
Bread for the World

PREFACE

From its inception this book has been a struggle and a joy—a struggle in that dealing with an issue so immense and complex has been like carrying the weight of the world on my shoulders. The more I know about how hunger happens and the suffering of individual persons, the more I feel their burden, and the more it seems that relief for all who hunger is a humanly impossible task—and it is, without God.

As I have written and spoken on this subject in my ministry, I have gone through periods of depression, guilt, frustration, and doubt both personally and professionally. In trying to organize and select this material, I have had the constant feeling that there is so much more to be said and done.

But there has been equal joy. In the last year churches around the world have begun to recognize the impact they can have on hunger issues and have begun to move, although there is still a long way to go. More individuals have a global consciousness and appreciation for their place in the world and their mission as Christians. Those who choose to care, care more deeply. This year I have experienced forgiveness, grace, assurance, and humor from God. I have grown in my understanding of myself, my world, and the depth of my faith. I humbly covet this growth for my fellow adventurers.

ACKNOWLEDGMENTS

I owe many people thanks.

To my mother and step-dad, Doris and Lyn Sims, my congregation in San Marcos, and the Board of Ordained Ministry of my annual conference for sharing my vision and financing my education, research, and writing.

To the late Charlie Guthrie for serving my church faithfully while I was on study leave.

To Janice Grana, Maxie Dunnam, and the Upper Room for risking faith in me.

To Dean Freudenberger for deepening and broadening my perspective and sharing his vision of a world without hunger.

To Marj Gatzke, my friend and co-worker on hunger, for continual help and support on the project.

To my children, Chris and Brian, for sacrificing many hours without me.

In gratitude to all, I give them the gift of hope.

TOM PETTEPIECE

INTRODUCTION

I came that they may have life, and have it abundantly.
JOHN 10:10*b*, (RSV)

Today a fully abundant life is beyond the reach of the majority of humanity. That two-thirds of the earth's people suffer from hunger either by starvation or malnutrition is an undeniable fact. Despite all else that troubles our planet, we live in a world hungry. It is a human condition Christians cannot ignore. As Christ's disciples we are called upon to respond urgently and effectively.

Hunger is a symptom of a greater malady. Our mission as believers is even more apparent when one considers that at the root of global and domestic hunger is a basic moral question of injustice.

The identifiable causes of hunger are varied and complex. Among the major ones are the following:

• The colonial legacy: nations conquered and subdued other nations to exploit their resources.

• Business expansion: multinational corporations are the new colonizers. Consumer demand in the rich nations means more exploitation of the hungry ones.

• Resource waste: the major waste of resources lies in the waste of soil and farmland and also in the waste of petroleum.

• Agricultural errors: improper farming methods and

15

technology used in the tropics are keeping the world hungry.

• Rural leadership vacuum: the colonial systems left the hungry nations with no real leadership as far as raising food.

• Urban growth: the concentration on cities and industrialization in the hungry world takes resources and priority away from the growth of food.

• Overpopulation: there is a disparity between the population growth rate and the production of food. The vital strategy for controlling population is fighting poverty and feeding the hungry.

• Military expansion: there is a preoccupation with defense spending and the arms race that is robbing the hungry world of its greatest security, sufficient food.*

The solutions to the hunger/justice issue are equally varied and multifaceted. This book lifts up many of the causes and beginning solutions for further consideration. But first, the more fundamental question—why respond? Why do Christians have a special concern and response to make?

The Bible is imperative—we are commanded to respond. And if, as believers, we are experiencing the gospel faithfully, we cannot help but respond. The writer of James gives us enough to meditate on for the whole subject when he says:

What does it profit, my brethren, if a man says he has faith but has not works? Can his faith save him? If a brother or sister is ill-clad and in lack of daily food, and one of you says to them, "Go in peace, be warmed and filled," without giving

---

*For a more detailed yet succinct account of the causes of hunger, see C. Dean Freudenberger and Paul Minus, *Christian Responsibility in a Hungry World* (Nashville: Abingdon, 1976).

them the things needed for the body, what does it profit? So faith by itself, if it has no works, is dead. For as the body apart from the spirit is dead, so faith apart from works is dead.

JAMES 2:14-17, 26, RSV

James considers it natural that a person with faith also has works. It is not a heavy and moralistic Christian duty; it is the Christian possibility and life-style—response comes with true faith.

On this theme, the Bible is clear and direct in both Testaments—God loves and cares for the poor. Jesus said to be perfect. In other words, to be imitators of the perfect God, to do as God does. If we are to love God, we are to love and care for the poor and hungry, too. "You will know them by their fruits" (Matt. 7:16a, RSV) he said, and he meant that we are known by our ethical behavior as illustrated by life experience.

According to a survey by a leading news magazine about institutions that have influence in society today, the church ranked nineteenth, just below the Republican Party in the aftermath of Watergate. If we have lost credibility in the eyes of those we serve, perhaps it is because we have lost sight of our biblical mandate to *do* as God does. Perhaps a way to gain it back is to respond with a renewed vision and purpose of meeting the basic needs of all of God's children.

Realistically, any response begins with where we are now and proceeds one step at a time. I suggest that we begin with our inner response and move on a continually interacting basis in the areas of study, prayer, and action.

First, *study.* Life informs our prayers; so our meditation and worship need to be informed, directed, and focused to become more meaningful. Study becomes a vital and effective part of our growing faith and response. While perhaps not "of" the world, we are called to live "in" the world, and an awareness of the facts and reality of our existence is a basic prerequisite to responsible Christian living. Tragically, too many Christians are biblically illiterate. How can we expect to integrate our faith and life without studying and internalizing our theological and biblical roots?

Each chapter in this book begins with some information designed to acquaint the reader with a topic related to the hunger issue, either as a cause or as part of the solution to the problem. The chapters demonstrate the interrelatedness and complexity of the issue, but are presented for individual consideration to help us deal constructively with an otherwise unmanageable subject and to focus our meditation and response on specifics.

Lest some persons find it hard to believe, all facts quoted, while not individually footnoted for space purposes, have been documented by at least two or more sources listed in the bibliography.

The scripture selections have been chosen with great care and speak to the major biblical themes of the Christian life-style and specifically to our missional response.

A study guide is provided for those individuals and groups who wish to pursue a more thorough study of both the facts and the biblical perspectives on the hunger/justice issue.

For those who choose, the material and prayers are appropriate for corporate worship as well. For years I have used a contemporary reading along with the scripture. Their complementary use or juxtaposition can be informative, insightful, and worshipful as it brings new awareness to both readings.

Second, *prayer.* Just as life informs our prayers, prayer informs our life.

INTRODUCTION

While I was writing this book, the pet kitten belonging to my five-year-old daughter, Chris, died; she was run over in the neighbor's driveway one morning. I found out about it before Chris did, so I was able to prepare her a little. Together we talked about God loving all living things, about my Dad who died before Chris was born, and about pets and accidents. When I told her about her kitty she didn't cry immediately.

We went outside and carried it to the garage. When Chris was back in her room lying on the bed, the tears came in a flood. I held her and we cried together, she for her kitty, I for both. Later, she watched me bury the kitten and helped me make a cross of wood. We said a prayer together and have every night since.

When life moves us, we pray. Even as children, it is part of our being. When confronted with disease and disaster, we pray.

Why a devotional book on hunger? We need to pray about a lot of things we do not know that much about. Yet, when confronted with the reality of hunger we cannot help but pray for its victims, whether they be the baby in the Sahel or the single parent next door who is too proud to apply for food stamps; and we pray for us, that we not be careless, unaware, and uncaring.

In Matthew we read:

Ask, and it will be given you; seek, and you will find; knock, and it will be opened to you. For every one who asks receives, and he who seeks finds, and to him who knocks it will be opened. Or what man of you, if his son asks him for bread, will give him a stone? Or if he asks for a fish, will give him a serpent? If you then, who are evil, know how to give good gifts to your children, how much more will your Father who is in heaven give good things to those who ask him!

MATTHEW 7:7-11, RSV

19

Jesus says, ask, seek, knock—do anything, but do pray! He tells us emphatically to pray because he knows we do not, that we doubt the power of prayer. He tells us to reassure us that our prayers are indeed heard. We should pray because in doing so our *real* needs are known and received, we find new growth and strength, new possibilities of living are opened up. We pray because, like the parent who lovingly provides for his children, we have complete confidence and trust that God gives what is good. If we know it to be true in life experience, how much more it is true for God.

Another reason to pray is that through prayer and worship we need to discover how to celebrate the Lord of our lives in the midst of a world hungry. Through prayer we can find a staying power for the struggle against hunger that will sustain us long after others have moved on to different issues and this one is still here.

Prayer is one of the oldest human behaviors. All people have done it. Like a baby needs to cry, we have a need to pray. At the very least, if we are not led to pray about hunger, something is wrong.

Third, *action*. The result of meaningful study and prayer is action. The discourse from Matthew quoted above ends with these familiar words:

So whatever you wish that men would do to you, do so to them; for this is the law and the prophets.

MATTHEW 7:12, RSV

As we are informed and as we acknowledge our humanness and dependence on our Creator, we are also freed for a new commitment and a renewed life-style of Christian witness. As Elizabeth O'Conner and others have demonstrated so vividly, quality time spent with God on the inward journey results in a stronger and more purposeful outward journey. As whole persons our life makes sense and is in harmony with the gospel when we allow time for both. They are inseparable as responses to God's great love.

The form, style, and magnitude of your action will vary with your ability and circumstances. The suggestions made at the end of each chapter are places to begin. They are things you can do and pray more about.

These three, *study, prayer,* and *action,* are all part of our response to a world hungry.

The purpose of this book, then, is for us all to know more about the biblical themes related to hunger, to be better informed about the issue itself, to pray for and with those who live with hunger daily, and prayerfully to consider our response as we meditate on these things.

This book does not have easy answers. There are too many self-help books today that speak a shallow and self-indulgent word. It is rather a devotional book to live with, one that should enable us to grow in practicing the presence of God in all of life.

❧ 1 ❧

ADVOCACY

For a politician to express an interest in the year 2000 is no longer regarded as evidence of impracticality or otherworldliness; it is a political plus.[1]

ALVIN TOFFLER,
AUTHOR AND PROFESSOR

RESOLVED That it is the sense of the Senate/House of Representatives that

1. Every person in this country and throughout the world has the right to food—the right to a nutritionally adequate diet—and that this right is henceforth to be recognized as a cornerstone of U. S. policy; and

2. This right become a fundamental point of reference in the formation of legislation and administrative decisions in areas such as trade, assistance, monetary reform, military spending and all other matters that bear on hunger; and

3. Concerning hunger in the United States we seek to enroll on food assistance programs all who are in need, to improve those programs and insure that recipients receive an adequate diet, and to attain full employment and a floor of economic decency for everyone; and

4. Concerning global hunger this country increase its assistance for self-help development among the world's poorest people. . . .

RIGHT-TO-FOOD RESOLUTION
as passed by the Congress
September 25, 1976

22

ADVOCACY

Can messages from ordinary citizens change decisions in Washington? The answer is an emphatic "Yes!" Don't let anyone tell you that members of Congress do not read their mail. They do, and they are influenced by what they read. . . . Thoughtfully presented points often tip a vote one way or another. Most Congress-persons receive only a handful of letters on any given issue. Often they receive none. They assume that each letter represents hundreds of other voters who don't bother to write. One letter can make a difference, and a dozen letters will make any member of Congress pay unusual attention.[2]

ARTHUR SIMON, DIRECTOR
Bread for the World

Watch out, for there will be men who will arrest you and take you to court, and they will whip you in the synagogues. For my sake you will be brought to trial before rulers and kings, to tell the Good News to them and to the Gentiles. When they bring you to trial, do not worry about what you are going to say or how you will say it; when the time comes, you will be given what you will say. For the words you speak will not be yours; they will come from the Spirit of your Father speaking through you.

Men will hand over their own brothers to be put to death, and fathers will do the same to their children; children will turn against their parents and have them put to death. Everyone will hate you because of me. But whoever holds out to the end will be saved. When they persecute you in one town, run away to another one. I assure you that you will not finish your work in all the towns of Israel before the Son of Man comes.

MATTHEW 10:17-23, TEV

Jesus said to them, "Render to Caesar the things that are Caesar's, and to God the things that are God's." And they were amazed at him.

MARK 12:17, RSV

23

VISIONS OF A WORLD HUNGRY

Lord, I know we cannot legislate love. So I used to think that Christians were wasting their time in the political world. But you have shown me otherwise.

You were born into the real world. You lived in that world so that the world might be saved through you. You called the church to be in the world—to live within the economic, social, and political systems in which it finds itself, and precisely in this arena to participate in the saving activity of God.

Yet, sometimes, because of the context of our world, I would like to forget all that, to retreat when things seem hopeless or difficult, to take the easy way out and just pay Caesar and forget that following you involves my whole life.

I am not a prophet, but sometimes the little I do seems hard. But I am comforted and encouraged by your word. A careful defense did not protect your followers, but they trusted you to help them speak the prophetic word.

They learned that a Christian cannot expect to be treated better than you were, that courageously following you may result in opposition anytime.

You did not separate sacred and secular nor divide ethics into political and religious. Well, I have written my legislators and gotten some dialogue in response.

And I am beginning to see that Christians can really make a difference by being advocates for public policy in a way that *does* help to legislate love and justice in the real world.

ADVOCACY

It is not perfect government we seek—but rather to bring our imperfections into conformity with your kingdom.

May we never lose sight of that.

Amen.

FOR FURTHER PRAYER AND ACTION

1. Start a hunger file; collect news articles and other material on hunger-related issues.
2. Join Bread for the World, Impact, WHEAT, or other organizations that lobby for the hungry.
3. Write your legislators. Ask what they are doing to help the hungry and poor, both domestically and globally.
4. Prayerfully support our political process and the elected and appointed leaders called upon to deal fairly and honestly with all.

2

CHILDREN

Severe undernutrition mainly strikes small children, who need about twice as much protein and energy in relation to overall body weight as adults require. Unfortunately, in many cultures a tradition of discriminating against small children and females of all ages in the allocation of family food supplies makes these two groups all the more vulnerable.

Undernutrition affects as many as half to two-thirds of the children in the poor countries. In many of the poorer countries, two-thirds of all deaths occur among children under five. . . . Undernutrition can injure even an unborn child. The influence can begin long before a child is even conceived. When a mother has been undernourished and unhealthy during her childhood, writes a prominent physician, "her pregnancy is more frequently disturbed and her child more often of low birth-weight. Thus undernutrition among girls today imperils the health of the next generation."[1]

> ERIK ECKHOLM AND
> FRANK RECORD
> *Worldwatch Institute*

A. C. Forrest is the editor of Canada's *United Church Observer*. He describes the following experience in Dhapa, India, a squalid slum outside Calcutta:

A pretty little Indian girl, 8 or 9 and naked except for some bracelets on her arm, was playing in a garbage can of water. I

CHILDREN

tossed her a small, very bouncy rubber ball, a number of which
I had purchased at the London airport to give to children. She
laughed and plunged her hand into the water where it had
fallen. When she retrieved it, a disappointed look crossed her
face. She couldn't eat it, and she didn't know what to do with
it. I gave no more toys to children in that hungry world.

The children beg for food, but no one gives to them.
LAMENTATIONS 4:4*b*, RSV

All through the night get up again and again to cry out to the
Lord;
Pour out your heart and beg him for mercy on your chil-
dren—
Children starving to death on every street corner!
Look, O Lord! Look at those you are making suffer!
Women are eating the bodies of the children they loved!
LAMENTATIONS 2:19-20*a*, TEV

When they had finished breakfast, Jesus said to Simon Peter, "Simon, son of John, do you love me more than these?" He
said to him, "Yes, Lord; you know that I love you." He said to
him, "Feed my lambs."
JOHN 21:15, RSV

**Lord, it seems incredibly unfair that the poor children
have to be the innocent victims.
They are so gentle, so naive, so helpless, so hopeful,
so responsive.
Yet they die first when hungry, or live half-lives
retarded or maimed from malnutrition.**

**They play in mudholes or wander the streets looking
for the love that died with their parents.**

27

VISIONS OF A WORLD HUNGRY

It makes me want to cry.
It hurts me to see the children divided by a world rich
and poor.

My own children are luckier.
In their pilgrimage through time they experience
playgrounds and balloons,
trips to buy candy and to the zoo,
pride at new discoveries and accomplishments,
smiles across the table,
kisses and snugglies at bedtime,
feelings of love and warmth,
their tummies full,
and their basic needs of life never questioned.

At times I have wanted to be a child again,
to relive happy and innocent days.
But it's harder to wish that now because the image of
the world's poor comes painfully to mind, and I feel
uneasy or afraid or angry.

Lord, help me resolve to act upon what really matters
in life, to respond in ways that reflect a sensitive
wondering and deep amazement at the value of every
life, always to hope, pray, and work so that all the
world's children may grow up liking who they are.

And help me to live so that my children won't also
think the world is unfair to children.
                                        Amen.

CHILDREN

FOR FURTHER PRAYER AND ACTION

1. Investigate what the high school in your area teaches about global development, if anything. Sponsor a food day there.
2. Teach, or support in some way, your church school where values for living can be taught.
3. Treat children as whole persons.
4. Make a poster or bulletin board for children that portrays some aspect of the hunger issue.
5. Play children's games from other lands.

❧ 3 ❧

COMMUNION

Today is Resurrection Sunday. My first Easter in prison. Surely the regime can't continue to keep almost 10,000 political prisoners in its gaols! In here, it is much easier to understand how the men in the Bible felt, stripping themselves of everything that was superfluous. Many of the prisoners have already heard that they have lost their homes, their furniture, and everything they owned. Our families are broken up. Many of our children are wandering the streets, their father in one prison, their mother in another.

There is not a single cup. But a score of Christian prisoners experienced the joy of celebrating communion—without bread or wine. The communion of empty hands. The non-Christians said: "We will help you; we will talk quietly so that you can meet." Too dense a silence would have drawn the guards' attention as surely as the lone voice of the preacher. "We have no bread, nor water to use instead of wine," I told them, "but we will act as though we had."

"This meal in which we take part," I said, "reminds us of the prison, the torture, the death and final victory of the resurrection of Jesus Christ. The bread is the body which He gave for humanity. The fact that we have none represents very well the lack of bread in the hunger of so many millions of human beings. The wine, which we don't have today, is His blood and represents our dream of a united humanity, of a just society, without difference of race or class."

I held out my empty hand to the first person on my right,

and placed it over his open hand, and the same with the others: "Take, eat, this is my body which is given for you; do this in remembrance of me." Afterward, all of us raised our hands to our mouths, receiving the body of Christ in silence. "Take, drink, this is the blood of Christ which was shed to seal the new covenant of God with men. Let us give thanks, sure that Christ is here with us, strengthening us."

We gave thanks to God, and finally stood up and embraced each other. A while later, another non-Christian prisoner said to me: "You people have something special, which I would like to have." The father of the dead girl came up to me and said: "Pastor, this was a real experience! I believe that today I discovered what faith is. Now, I believe that I am on the road."[1]

Excerpted from
a report from Latin America

The word *communicate* (from the Latin *commune*) means to share, to exchange, to relate, to live together, to participate, to converse, to have something in common. From the same root come communion, commune, community. It has the same meaning as *koinonia* in the New Testament, which refers both to communion with Christ—to the point of sharing in his passion and death—and communion with each other, both in spiritual and in material gifts.[2]

MORTIMER ARIAS, FORMER BISHOP,
Methodist Church in Bolivia

While they were eating, Jesus took a piece of bread, gave a prayer of thanks, broke it, and gave it to his disciples. "Take it," he said, "this is my body."

Then he took a cup, gave thanks to God, and handed it to them; and they all drank from it. Jesus said, "This is my blood which is poured out for many, my blood which seals God's covenant. I tell you, I will never again drink this wine until the day I drink the new wine in the Kingdom of God."

MARK 14:22-25, TEV

Jesus said to them, "Come and eat." None of the disciples dared ask him, "Who are you?" because they knew it was the Lord. So Jesus went over, took the bread, and gave it to them; he did the same with the fish.

This, then, was the third time Jesus appeared to the disciples after he was raised from death.

JOHN 21:12-14, TEV

Because there is one bread, we who are many are one body, for we all partake of the one bread.

1 CORINTHIANS 10:17, RSV

Lord, you are the bread of life, the manna, the
God-providing-sustenance for life.
Just as you were known to your disciples in the
breaking of bread, you come vividly to mind as I take
this bread and cup.

I am reminded that you summed up the whole
meaning of your life and death in the sharing of this
food, that communion is not only about eating but
sharing.

Lord, to be human is to be hungry. Not to be is to be
dead. But sometimes with my high standard of living I
forget, not only about the painful experience of the
physical hunger of others in which their human
dimensions lie dormant, but of my own hungers as well.

Sometimes in my comfortableness
I forget, for a moment, about my deep need for the
authentic love which gives me a foundation for
personal worth and meaning, one not dependent on
things, but on the only thing that matters—my
relationship to you.

COMMUNION

As I eat and drink, I remember that you have become
the Bread of Life for me as I have lived for others and
found fulfillment of my own being, and that only
through this way of living has my hunger for authentic
love truly been fed.

Yes, you are known in the breaking of bread. And I
pray that as I commune with you in this act, and in life,
I would more deeply know what it means to share in
the depth of your life and death as I am in communion
with my sisters and brothers.

Amen.

FOR FURTHER PRAYER AND ACTION

1. Encourage your pastor to include hymns, readings,
   and scripture related to hunger in worship.
2. Write your own prayer for the hungry and share it.
3. Have a "communion of empty hands" in your church or
   with your family.
4. Share a meal with a lonely or needy person in your
   church or neighborhood.

✿ 4 ✿

COMMUNITY

Political scientists have long known that community in all its forms can play a key role in the distribution of power. Families, neighborhoods, work teams, church and other voluntary associations mediate between the lone individual and the power of the state. They provide the person with a human buffer zone so that he or she does not stand alone against the state's demands. They amplify the individual's small voice so that it can be heard by a state which can turn deaf when it does not want to listen.[1]

PARKER J. PALMER
DEAN OF STUDIES, *Pendle Hill*

Each element of our current concerns—energy, population, the environment, food supply—confirms the interrelatedness of the human condition and the planetary convergence of our national destinies. It is not now so much the moral perception that we are each our brother's keeper, but the practical reality that each brother is our keeper. National self-interest demands an international restructuring that acknowledges this reality of our human condition.[2]

SHRIDATH S. RAMPHAL,
COMMONWEALTH
SECRETARY-GENERAL, *Guyana*

The Church . . . has a unique role to play, for the estrangement experienced by modern humanity flows fundamentally from the loss of true community. That is what the band of

34

those committed to the Good News can restore. A beginning
point for their witness is the setting forth of a model for community which rests on new values and embodies the first signs
of a New Order in the world. Economically, socially, racially,
and spiritually, such new communities can point the way to the
rest of the world, and become true means of hope for us all to
build a future of promise and creativity.[3]

MARK HATFIELD, U. S. SENATOR

Genuine community is the highest achievement of humankind, demands more of us than any other endeavor, and is
supremely worth the struggle.[4]

ELIZABETH O'CONNER,
Church of the Savior

They spent their time in learning from the apostles, taking
part in the fellowship, and sharing in the fellowship meals and
the prayers. . . .
All the believers continued together in close fellowship and
shared their belongings with one another. They would sell
their property and possessions, and distribute the money
among all, according to what each one needed. Day after day
they met as a group in the Temple, and they had their meals
together in their homes, eating with glad and humble hearts,
praising God, and enjoying the good will of all the people.

ACTS 2:42, 44-47a, TEV

We love because God first loved us. If someone says he loves
God, but hates his brother, he is a liar. For he cannot love God,
whom he has not seen, if he does not love his brother, whom he
has seen. The command that Christ has given us is this: whoever loves God must love his brother also.

1 JOHN 4:19-21, TEV

I am not trying to relieve others by putting a burden on you;
but since you have plenty at this time, it is only fair that you
should help those who are in need. Then, when you are in need

and they have plenty, they will help you. In this way both are treated equally. As the scripture says, "The one who gathered much did not have too much, and the one who gathered little did not have too little."

2 CORINTHIANS 8:13-15, TEV

"I pray that they may all be one. Father! May they be in us, just as you are in me and I am in you. May they be one, so that the world will believe that you sent me."

JOHN 17:21, TEV

A man stood up in the back and asked the speaker if he was a Communist. I couldn't believe it. One of the most articulate, sensitive, and experienced experts on hunger, twenty-seven years a missionary, had just spoken on the moral perspectives of sharing the earth's resources among the two-thirds of humanity living in poverty, and this man asks if he is a Communist.

Lord, you prayed that we would all be one. The longer I live, the more convinced I am that it is only as we are one in you that we have a chance of that coming true.

I become frustrated as community seems to elude me until I remember that it was not the unity of human organization you meant, but rather the divine gift of fellowship with you.

Today we live in an interdependent world. Nations and corporations who use freedom to exploit the world for their own gain, not thinking of others, shatter the fragile web of interrelationship and community now beginning to encircle all humanity.

In addition to the church there is at least one worldwide organization that furthers community as it

36

deepens human understanding—the United Nations.
Those who advocate its dismantling are as
narrow-minded as the man who shouted,
"Communist."

They forget, or don't know, that this international
community supplies vaccines that stamp out smallpox
and malaria, helps the homeless and the hungry,
protects millions from blindness, responds to disaster,
reduces illiteracy, provides clean water, safeguards
air safety, helps keep the peace, promotes
self-development, and more.

As part of the community of humanity, the world *is* my
business. And while I see no perfect human peace and
solution to our disparity, I see many hopeful signs of
your love.

Because I am part of the community of the church, the
quality of life in this world is also my business. And as
part of the fellowship that proclaims you as the hope
of the world, I, too, pray that we may all be one.
Amen.

FOR FURTHER PRAYER AND ACTION

1. Suggest that students choose a pen pal in a Third
   World country.
2. Request a hunger book display in your public library.
3. Start a community food pantry at your church. Make it
   ecumenical.
4. Encourage the community groups to which you belong
   to have a program on hunger and/or donate funds to
   hunger causes.
5. Have a neighborhood garage sale and donate some of
   the proceeds to a hunger-related cause.

❧ 5 ❧

CREATION

Since creation began, there have always been crises of one kind or another affecting human life, but there has been an underlying harmony and confidence that nature would restore order by itself. Now, however, the two worlds of our existence, the biosphere of our inheritance and the technosphere of our own creation, are out of balance and are potentially in very deep conflict. We have reached the point where we have the capacity to permanently alter the interrelationship of human life and our natural life support systems.

As Rene Dubos and Barbara Ward said in *Only One Earth,* "This is the hinge of history at which we stand, the door of the future opening on to a crisis more sudden, more global, more inescapable, and more bewildering than any ever encountered by the human species and one which will take decisive shape within the life span of children who are already born."[1]

Life itself is under threat, both the quality of life such as it is *and* sheer survival. Our minimal goals must be the removal of the threat to sheer survival and to the deterioration of the quality of life of the inhabitants of this earth, especially the poor. So a prior requirement of any global society is that it be so organized that the life of man and other living creatures on

CREATION

which his life depends can be sustained indefinitely within the limits of the earth. A second requirement is that it be sustained at a quality that makes possible fulfillment of human life for all people.[2]

CHARLES BIRCH, BIOLOGIST,
Sidney University

O Lord, our Lord,
    how majestic is thy name in all the
        earth!

Thou whose glory above the heavens
        is chanted
    by the mouth of babes and infants,
thou hast founded a bulwark be-
        cause of thy foes,
    to still the enemy and the avenger.

When I look at thy heavens, the
        work of thy fingers,
    the moon and the stars which
        thou hast established;
what is man that thou art mindful
        of him,
    and the son of man that thou dost
        care for him?

Yet thou hast made him little less
        than God,
    and dost crown him with glory
        and honor.
Thou hast given him dominion over
        the works of thy hands;
    thou hast put all things under his
        feet,
all sheep and oxen,
    and also the beasts of the field,

the birds of the air, and the fish of
the sea,
whatever passes along the paths
of the sea.

O Lord, our Lord,
how majestic is thy name in all
the earth!

PSALM 8, RSV

And God saw everything that he had made, and behold, it
was very good.

GENESIS 1:31*a*, RSV

O God, who creates and is always creating the sphere
of our very life, I thank you for your life-giving and
sustaining presence, the gift of this magnificent earth,
and the ability to use and reshape its resources to
meet our needs.

I confess that I have ignored sometimes our being too
enterprising with your creation, so that now people
are hungry because we have mismanaged our finite
world. Our vision has been shallow, and we have not
always seen that too much for some really means too
little for others.

God, help me to act responsibly by treating the crisis
of sustainability as an opportunity for positive action.
Save us from a plundered planet. Rather, enable us
not only to meet the "inner limits" of human need, but
to do so without stepping over the "outer-limits" of
our biosphere's tolerance.

40

CREATION

Help us to act as though we, the world's people together, have received a precious gift from you to be appreciated and shared by all.

Amen.

FOR FURTHER PRAYER AND ACTION

1. How does the concern for renewability fit into God's scheme of creation?
2. It has been said, "Where there is no vision the people perish." What is God's vision for creation in the Bible?
3. What seems to be ours?
4. How and why are they different?
5. How can we act to make them the same?

≈ 6 ≈

ECONOMICS

One historical root cause of hunger is the 300-year legacy of colonialism. Lands conquered by powerful nations became colonies that were used to grow nonfood items for export. The agricultural, social, cultural, and economic systems of the people became centered on producing goods desired back home—rubber, cocoa, tea, coffee, cotton, timber, sugar, peanuts, and others.

By the late sixties, most of the colonies had obtained political independence, but they remained saddled with the old economic systems based on export and mining. Today it is extremely difficult, if not impossible, for these new nations, regardless of their political ideologies, to make rapid agricultural transitions to grow food crops. Without massive help the result is hunger and famine.

Expansion in the last decade of multinational corporations, which are based in the wealthy nations and operate in the poor nations, has continued unprecedented demands on natural resources of the former colonies. In addition, through skillful advertising demand is created for consumer items which disrupt the social, cultural, and economic life of the people by diverting resources needed for food and other basics of a decent standard of living.

Most Americans (87 percent) favor direct aid to poor nations in the form of medicine, food, educational and technical assistance, and disaster relief. And most think that the United States leads the world in aid.

The reality is that out of seventeen nations listed by the World Bank as giving developmental assistance, the U.S. ranks fourteenth with only .23 of 1% of Gross National Product going for aid, and much of that is either tied to political considerations or is in the form of military assistance. Our assistance is less than one-tenth the level it was at the end of World War II. It is not a record of which we should be proud.

Trade is a hunger issue also. The share of world trade for poor countries has steadily declined, while their international debts have steadily risen. These countries need fairer trade arrangements if they are to invest in rural development and feed their people.

This is how the judgment works: the light has come into the world, but people love the darkness rather than the light, because their deeds are evil. Anyone who does evil things hates the light and will not come to the light, because he does not want his evil deeds to be shown up. But whoever does what is true comes to the light in order that the light may show that what he did was in obedience to God.

JOHN 3:19-21, TEV

He also said to them, "Pay attention to what you hear! The same rules you use to judge others will be used by God to judge you—but with even greater severity. The person who has something will be given more, and the person who has nothing will have taken away from him even the little he has."

MARK 4:24-25, TEV

And he answered them, "He who has two coats, let him share with him who has none; and he who has food, let him do likewise."

LUKE 3:11, RSV

Command those who are rich in the things of this life not to be proud, but to place their hope, not in such an uncertain thing as riches, but in God, who generously gives us everything for our enjoyment. Command them to do good, to be rich in good works, to be generous and ready to share with others. In this way they will store up for themselves a treasure which will be a solid foundation for the future. And then they will be able to win the life which is true life.

1 Timothy 6:17-19, tev

Lord, someone once said that you could tell a lot about a person's character and loyalties by looking at his or her checkbook. It must be true, for you told us many times that the way we use money measures our values. You warned your followers against the vice of avarice—the desire to get and keep money, the greed for riches.

Today you challenge our hypocrisy. You call our institutions to serve human need, not partisan interests. You call us to value persons, not to exploit them for the sake of economic gain.

You call us to concern for the needy, not the pursuit of higher interest rates. You lead us to protest injustice and not complacently assume that the marketplace will make ethical choices by itself.

Lord, it seems that hunger and other degrading human conditions should not be tolerated, especially in the United States, not to mention the rest of the world's countries, most of which are a great deal poorer.

It seems that the purpose of any economic system should be to promote and enhance the dignity and well-being of *each* member of society, and that if the institutions involved in that system are not promoting the common good of the people, they should be changed.

Right now it is unfair that only about 6 percent of the world's people (myself included) consume over 40 percent of its goods and services. It is unfair that international trade agreements help keep poor people in debt, and thereby hungry.

As a Christian, and as a member of the wealthiest nation on earth, I cannot responsibly ignore how economic systems affect the lives of others.

Lord, I want to believe that systems made by people can be changed by people for the better. I want to work for a more just and human society. I want to affirm that your example of simpler living is not only ethically sound but is actually a requisite for survival today.

And as I make choices about what to write checks for, help me keep in mind it is not things but *people* who really matter.

Amen.

FOR FURTHER PRAYER AND ACTION

1. When you hear about a company that exploits people or resources in developing countries, let them know you will not give them your business.
2. Set an amount in your own budget to go to hunger-related causes.
3. Help eliminate trade deficits in hungry nations by buying their products.
4. Protest exploitation of cheap labor by multinationals in foreign nations by boycotting their products. Tell them why you are doing so.

~ 7 ~

ENVIRONMENT

What hurts is to be driving in the countryside, turn the corner and suddenly come upon the earth being cut, clawed, scraped, and rearranged by giant yellow machines where only last week there had been chaparral. Last time it happened I slowed down and drove by with my mouth literally open in amazement at the vast area of red earth being exposed. It reminded me of an operation performed without anesthesia, for it appeared as if the earth itself was bleeding and crying out in pain.

Now, I am not an ecology "nut," as some would say, and I am not against new housing. However, I am a strong supporter of conservation and sensible land use and maintaining the renewability of our environment for all to use. From my office adjacent to what appears to be acres of lifeless, "unused" land, I have come to know an abundance of life. Quail and their chicks, roadrunners, rabbits, squirrels, lizards, and birds are just a few. They were the first thing that entered my mind as I turned the corner that day. I thought, "How silly. I'm feeling like a little child crying over his dead frog or something. Who cares about a few little animals in the vastness of this world?"

Ah, yes. That *is* the question. Who *does* care about them? And more specifically about the way we abuse our resources.

47

Picture Jesus today standing on that hill about to address a crowd. "Consider the lilies . . . er, ah . . . well, then consider the birds . . . er, ah. . . ." What would he say today about the whole thing?

One of the many groups concerned about environmental quality is called Friends of the Earth. I am not a member, but I like that thought—being a friend of the earth—especially when I consider that God entrusted it to me. In this day and age it seems that the earth could use a few friends.

The fear of you and the dread of you shall be upon every beast of the earth, and upon every bird of the air, upon everything that creeps on the ground and all the fish of the sea; into your hand they are delivered. Every moving thing that lives shall be food for you; and as I gave you the green plants, I give you everything.

GENESIS 9:2-3, RSV

The land which you are going over to possess is a land of hills and valleys, which drinks water by the rain from heaven, a land which the Lord your God cares for; the eyes of the Lord your God are always upon it, from the beginning of the year to the end of the year.

DEUTERONOMY 11:11-12, RSV

The Lord is gracious and merciful,
    slow to anger and abounding in steadfast love.
The Lord is good to all,
    and his compassion is over all that he has made.

PSALM 145:8-9, RSV

God, I am grateful that at least the awareness of the condition of our environment has had enough publicity to be of some public interest, but I am still dismayed

48

that nations and individuals do not act more in
accordance with our interrelatedness to it.

Climates are changing partly because literally no
place on earth is free from the effects of pollution.
Irresponsible destruction of agricultural land, erosion,
deforestation, desertification, and other resource
abuses continue because of ignorance, social neglect,
and ruthless profit motives. Energy and fertilizer
costs keep rising as demand increases and we run out
of nonrenewable resources.

It seems that some think we can mortgage the future
by trading off the environment for immediate jobs or
monetary gain. That certainly has little to do with the
biblical perspective of sensitivity to all life, being at
peace with our environment, the norm of social justice
and human dignity.

God, I try to take responsibility for using energy and
other resources wisely in my personal life. But if I can
do one other thing of value, perhaps it will be to
further articulate the vision you have given us of
environmental sustainability, understanding about
love and your kingdom on earth.

Perhaps I can help others see that environmental
quality and energy use is not a partisan issue—but a
human and global issue, and that we *do* live in one
world. From that perspective perhaps we will more
diligently seek responsible land use, appropriate
technology, and responsible national policies which
affect hungry people.

God, our dependence on rain, oil, and other gifts of the
earth should remind us of our dependence on you.
Forgive us for not being more perceptive of that. I am
grateful that you remember we are frail, needy, and
erring, and you still have compassion. I am grateful,
too, for your mercy and abundance of steadfast love.

May the way I live in your world reflect my gratitude.
Amen.

FOR FURTHER PRAYER AND ACTION

1. Plant a seed tree.
2. When you can, walk or ride a bike or the bus instead of
   driving.
3. Take seriously the idea that you should consume less
   water and energy in your home.
4. Take seriously the respect for natural ecological systems.

☙ 8 ❧

FOOD

The act of putting into your mouth what the earth has
grown is perhaps your most direct interaction with the earth.[1]

FRANCES MOORE LAPPÉ

For the first time in history we can see a connection
between the eating habits of U. S. citizens and hunger for
millions of others. On the average each person in the United
States consumes about 1,850 pounds of grain a year, most of it
in the form of meat and dairy products. The average in poor
countries is about 400 pounds—almost all of it consumed directly. Seven pounds of grain go into the average pound of
edible beef, according to the U. S. Department of Agriculture.
Hungry people see our heavy meat diet taking a disproportionate share of the world food supply.[2]

An Alternate Diet

The victim of starvation burns up his own body fats, muscles
and tissues for fuel. His body quite literally consumes itself
and deteriorates rapidly. The kidneys, liver and endocrine
system often cease to function properly. A shortage of car-
bohydrates, which play a vital role in brain chemistry, affects
the mind. Lassitude and confusion set in, so that starvation
victims often seem unaware of their plight. The body's de-
fenses drop; disease kills most famine victims before they have
time to starve to death. An individual begins to starve when

he has lost about a third of his normal body weight. Once this loss exceeds 40 per cent, death is almost inevitable.

TIME MAGAZINE
November 11, 1974

In June of 1976, I attended the World Food Conference in Ames, Iowa. Scientists from seventy nations representing both the developed and developing world converged to talk about the future of food. Experts in all fields related to food spoke, discussed, and debated, but none disagreed that the world is now, and in the future, capable of growing enough food to feed even the rapidly growing population. Technically it can be done. It is the economic, social, and political dimensions of food that keep people hungry.

Yet there is a tremendous misconception still prevalent that hunger is only a matter of solving the "food problem," especially among the scientific and university community as evidenced in Ames. There is an urgent need to bring together those who are working on the "food problem" with those who see the question as the "hunger issue." The real future of food involves both.

There in the desert they all complained to Moses and Aaron and said to them, "We wish that the Lord had killed us in Egypt. There we could at least sit down and eat meat and as much other food as we wanted. But you have brought us out into this desert to starve us all to death."

The Lord said to Moses, "Now I am going to cause food to rain down from the sky for all of you. The people must go out every day and gather enough for that day. In this way I can test them to find out if they will follow my instructions."

"I have heard the complaints of the Israelites. Tell them that at twilight they will have meat to eat, and in the morning they

FOOD

will have all the bread they want. Then they will know that I, the Lord, am their God."

EXODUS 16:2-4, 12, TEV

Those who died in the war
were better off than those
who died later,
who starved slowly to death,
with no food to keep them alive.

The disaster that came to my
people brought horror;
loving mothers boiled their
own children for food.

LAMENTATIONS 4:9-10, TEV

Jesus called his disciples to him and said, "I feel sorry for these people, because they have been with me for three days and now have nothing to eat. I don't want to send them away without feeding them, for they might faint on their way home."

The disciples asked him, "Where will we find enough food in this desert to feed this crowd?"

"How much bread do you have?" Jesus asked.

"Seven loaves," they answered, "and a few small fish."

So Jesus ordered the crowd to sit down on the ground. Then he took the seven loaves and the fish, gave thanks to God, broke them, and gave them to the disciples; and the disciples gave them to the people. They all ate and had enough. Then the disciples took up seven baskets full of pieces left over. The number of men who ate was four thousand, not counting the women and children.

MATTHEW 15:32-38, TEV

Food. We preserve, emulsify, thicken, thin, flavor, enhance, sweeten, age, oxidize, color, bake, boil, fry, blend, process, box, wrap, dehydrate, and freeze it.

VISIONS OF A WORLD HUNGRY

We also waste it. *O Stod.*

Every year literally millions of tons of food are thrown away in restaurants, supermarkets, homes, and institutions. Millions more are dumped rotten or insect-infested because of lack of proper storage, shipping, and distribution methods.

In a world hungry, Lord, I must ask am I guilty?

Food.

As a North American I eat about five times as much grain as a person in the Third World, three times as much fat and sugar, twelve times as much meat, yet, as a percentage of my income, spend four times *less* for food than my poorer sister and brother.

In a world hungry, Lord, I must confess, I am guilty. But I am also changing. I purposely eat less meat, sugar, and saturated fats and eat more grains, fruits, and vegetables. I eat fewer meals. I patronize fast food chains less. I try to spend less overall for food and send the difference plus some to support those who need more food.

These are only beginnings and I am not proud, but I am probably healthier—physically, mentally, and spiritually. I am not absolved, but I am probably more aware on a daily basis of the precious gift of food and that taking it for granted is a luxury I can no longer afford.

Lord, I did not plan to be an overconsumer or to be a glutton, or to use more than my share of your bounty.

FOOD

And I do not need to respond out of guilt for that. For
you accept me for who I am, and forgive my
shortcomings and failures. That is precisely why I am
able to persevere with strength and hope in the fight
against hunger and the attempt to use responsibly
that precious commodity—food. *Amen.*

FOR FURTHER PRAYER AND ACTION

1. Put the topic of hunger on your family supper agenda.
2. Set an empty place at the table to represent the hungry. Do it weekly adding parts of a table service each time.
3. Designate certain days as meatless for you.
4. Evaluate your menu and cut out all unnecessary snack foods.

❦ 9 ❧

FREEDOM

The violation of any right that keeps any human being from the abundant life promised and fulfilled in Jesus Christ is, therefore, not just a crime against humanity but defiance against God himself.[1]

HUMAN RIGHTS BACKGROUND
DOCUMENT
*Commission of the Churches on
International Affairs of the
World Council of Churches*

It is a cock-eyed view that regards ecological liberation as a distraction from the task of liberation of the poor. One cannot be done without the other. It is time to recognize that the liberation movement is finally one movement. It includes women's liberation, men's liberation, the liberation of science and technology, animal liberation, plant liberation and the liberation of the air and the oceans, the forests, deserts, mountains and valleys.[2]

CHARLES BIRCH, BIOLOGIST,
Sydney University

There is a *convergence* today between the Biblical view of Jesus as Liberator, and the cry of oppressed peoples for liberation. For our own day, to "see the world through eyes other than our own" has simply got to mean seeing it through the eyes of the poor and dispossessed. When the story of Jesus and the story of human oppression are put side by side, they *fit*.

FREEDOM

They are simply different versions of the same story. The cry of the hungry is overwhelming. The cry of the politically and economically exploited is overwhelming. The cry of those in prison and under torture is overwhelming. The cry of parents who know that their children are doomed to stunted and warped lives is overwhelming. . . . There may have been other emphases needed at other points in Christian history when talking about Jesus as Liberator, but I am persuaded that for *this* time and *this* place, the claim of Jesus to bring freedom, and the cry of oppressed peoples for freedom, converge and cannot be separated.[3]

ROBERT MCAFEE BROWN,
PROFESSOR
Union Theological Seminary

The Lord feeds the hungry
   and sets the prisoner free.
The Lord restores sight to the blind
   and straightens backs which are bent;
the Lord loves the righteous
   and watches over the stranger;
the Lord gives heart to the orphan and widow
but turns the course of the wicked to their ruin.

PSALM 146:7-9, NEB

Do not cheat a poor and needy hired servant, whether he is a fellow Israelite or a foreigner living in one of your towns. Each day before sunset pay him for that day's work; he needs the money and has counted on getting it. If you do not pay him, he will cry out against you to the Lord, and you will be guilty of sin.

Never forget that you were slaves in Egypt; that is why I have given you this command.

DEUTERONOMY 24:14-15,22, TEV

He who closes his ear to the cry of the poor will himself cry out and not be heard.

PROVERBS 21:13, RSV

57

VISIONS OF A WORLD HUNGRY

So if the Son makes you free, you will be free indeed.
JOHN 8:36, RSV

In 1776 our country *fought* to be free from oppression,
to be independent, to obtain human rights. For more
than two hundred years we have justified that fight for
freedom. Yet today we too easily condemn others who
want to be free. In Old Testament times the whole
economy was for supplying peoples' needs, and special
attention was given to the welfare of the weak and
poor. The focus of God's law was not on the rights of
the strong, but of the weak which the strong were
inclined to neglect or deny. Yet too easily we forget
that freedom means responsibility.

You created me in freedom, Lord. You redeemed me
to be free. Today the world is full of democratic
constitutions and bills of rights that bear little
resemblance to the economic, social, and political
realities which oppress many peoples. Help me to do
my homework on these inequalities and support
policies that overcome them.

Today too much of my country's investment in foreign
economies has been heedless of the cost to human
freedom and rights. Help me support an approach
which acknowledges that true freedom is inseparably
linked to all other human rights and means nothing
without the right to life, health, food, assembly,
education, press and more.

As a Christian, my approach to freedom must insist on
the embodiment of holiness in the physical conditions
of life. I must be committed to making rights matter,

FREEDOM

especially when I know that the violation of these
rights helps keep people hungry.

May I look with the eyes of Jesus and see what the
world cannot see. May I proclaim boldly that the
gospel has the seeds of freedom in it.

Amen.

FOR FURTHER PRAYER AND ACTION

1. In light of your knowledge and understanding of early
   United States history, rethink your feelings about
   Third World liberation movements.
2. Pray for innocent victims of torture and other acts of
   oppression.
3. Support efforts to affirm human rights.
4. Remember that underneath all labels and names given
   to political groups are persons of worth and value who
   are loved by God and should be loved and prayed for
   by us.

❦ 10 ❧

GROWTH

"Earthkeeping" on public television once aired a segment on megalopolises to explore the question of whether we will revamp our existing large cities or build new planned communities as demands for housing and services increase with population. It is a problem our generation will have to answer.

I was cheering as developers, city planners, and environmentalists alike gave priority to the quality of human life. Space, green belts, uninterrupted pedestrain and bicycle paths, central shopping coupled with the latest in people-movers, schools, hospitals, and communications in one totally planned community.

The architect continued to explain the plan: "Here in this triangular space (roughly 120 yards on the side) will be the center of the community. There will be a large circular tower about thirty feet in diameter standing sixty feet tall. Its base will be sculptured and on top will be the telecommunications antennas symbolically tying the community together. That's where the church tower used to stand." I stopped cheering.

Historically it was true. The church used to be the center not only of people's religious life, but also their social, cultural, and sometimes economic and political life. It was the community gathering place, the communications center so to speak. Today things have changed, and it was not that I objected to. The architect's plan was symbolic of a more serious defect of our urbanized way of life.

We talk of the development of people and the growth of community yet ignore or relegate to low priority the things which we all know are necessary to the development of the whole person and the establishment of true and lasting community.

Indiscriminate growth sometimes means growth without careful regard for the spiritual values fundamental to the basic needs of persons.

Concern for "quality of life," yet no mention was ever made in the program of a religious center of *any* kind, not to mention the Christian church. What kind of automatons are expected to live in "planned" communities where no one has a need for God?

Presently, developers are determining the destiny of our remaining resources without historical and cultural perspectives, and certainly without deeper spiritual values. It is crucial that these decisions be made on the basis of broader human values—values that relate to space, the room to wander, and to be stimulated by the Creation. Such decisions cannot be made purely on the basis of profit and loss. Far broader intangible values must be brought into account, and this can be done only by the input of those from many walks of life who have a concern for the whole person.[1]

MARK HATFIELD, U. S. SENATOR

Then said Jesus to the crowds and to his disciples, "The scribes and the Pharisees sit on Moses' seat; so practice and observe whatever they tell you, but not what they do; for they preach, but do not practice. They bind heavy burdens, hard to bear, and lay them on men's shoulders; but they themselves will not move them with their finger. They do all their deeds to be seen by men; for they make their phylacteries broad and their fringes long, and they love the place of honor at feasts and the best seats in the synagogues, and salutations in the market places and being called rabbi by men. But you are not to be called rabbi, for you have one teacher, and you are all brethren. And call no man your father on earth, for you have one Father, who is in heaven. Neither be called masters, for you have one master, the Christ. He who is greatest among you shall be your servant; whoever exalts himself will be humbled, and whoever humbles himself will be exalted.

MATTHEW 23:1-12, RSV

Listen to this, you that trample on the needy and try to destroy the poor of the country. You say to yourselves, "We can hardly wait for the holy days to be over so that we can sell our grain. When will the Sabbath end, so that we can start selling again? Then we can overcharge, use false measures, and fix the scales to cheat our customers. We can sell worthless wheat at a high price. We'll find a poor man who can't pay his debts, not even the price of a pair of sandals, and we'll buy him as a slave."

The Lord, the God of Israel, has sworn, "I will never forget their evil deeds."

AMOS 8:4-7, TEV

Lord, I guess there is no question that things are going to keep expanding, simply because there are more and more people. We need more houses, streets, stores, industry, cars, schools, and hospitals to meet peoples' needs.

And as I think about growth, that is the thing I need to pray about—does the growth really meet peoples' needs? To grow food better some farmers in the topics don't need bigger tractors and combines. They need

better hand tools and small machinery to work their kind of land in their kind of place.

To provide better incomes for the poor in developing countries, sometimes they don't need a bigger factory, but more credit for small businesses which support the local economy. To preserve community we often don't need standardization, but creativity with integrity as we zone and plan our cities.

Surely compromises must be made so no one gets hurt. But if we've learned anything, we know that growth by itself does not mean progress. It is only such when coupled with hard questioning of facts and an honest assessment of how human values and needs are being met.

Of course, Lord, that is a matter of judgment, so I look to you for guidance. You criticized the Pharisees for not practicing what they preach. I stand under that same judgment. Amos warned of the wicked who exploit their control and power. I don't know any people advocating growth who are purposely wicked, but I do know many who have control and power. I pray that you would give them strength and vision before they act to consider *all* the peoples' needs, especially the poor and powerless.

And, Lord, may I not just be an armchair critic of growth, but risk being in dialogue with those who make decisions, so that together we may grow in our understanding of what it means to enhance quality of life.

Amen.

FOR FURTHER PRAYER AND ACTION

1. Evaluate how your own immediate neighborhood and community could be improved to enhance everyone's quality of life.
2. Attend a planning commission or city council meeting in your town. What values seem to be used to determine growth patterns?
3. Give to rural development projects either domestically or internationally which increase employment in the rural sector.
4. Reflect on what part your job plays in growth to meet affluent desires or growth to meet human needs.

❧ II ❧

HEALTH

The basic source of ill health for humanity is malnutrition, and today it wears two faces—undernutrition for the poor and overnutrition for the affluent.

Of the world's poor, 1,600 million lack access to proper health care. Seventy percent are without a safe and dependable water supply. One-fourth of all the world's deaths are children under five years of age and undernutrition has a hand in most of them. Life expectancy in Africa is forty-three, Asia fifty-five, the developed world seventy-one. Twenty to one hundred thousand children lose their sight completely every year for want of vitamin A. Many suffer irreversible brain damage. People who are undernourished and in ill health are often too fatigued to work.

For the overnourished, an affluent diet and life-style contribute to ill health. Crowding, pollution, industrial hazards, indiscriminate economic growth, overly processed foods and sedentary life-styles all contribute to poor health. Heart disease is the cause of about half of all deaths in industrialized countries. Respiratory and cardiovascular diseases are increasing, as are hypertension, atherosclerosis, cancer, and dental cares, not to mention obesity, alcoholism, mental illness, stress-related diseases, and accidents.

VISIONS OF A WORLD HUNGRY

There is a health concept in medicine as old as the Hebrews in the Bible—treat the whole person, mind, body, and spirit.

For rich and poor it involves modifying today's living conditions. For the poor specifically, it means more than increasing appropriate medical services, though they are needed. It means social and economic development to provide nutritious food, clean water, proper housing, family planning, participation of rural communities in securing health services and other facilities.

Ministering to the whole person, including their health, is part of the good news Jesus had in mind for all persons. Affirming that is part of responding to a world hungry.

Give justice to the weak and the fatherless;
    maintain the right of the afflicted and the destitute.
Rescue the weak and the needy;
    deliver them from the hand of the wicked."

They have neither knowledge nor understanding,
    they walk about in darkness;
    all the foundations of the earth are shaken.
                                        PSALM 82:3-5, RSV

My dear friend, I pray that everything may go well with you and that you may be in good health—as I know you are well in spirit. I was so happy when some Christian brothers arrived and told me how faithful you are to the truth—just as you always live in the truth. Nothing makes me happier than to hear that my children live in the truth.
                                        3 JOHN 1:2-4, TEV

And Jesus went about all the cities and villages, teaching in their synagogues and preaching the gospel of the kingdom, and healing every disease and every infirmity. When he saw the crowds, he had compassion for them, because they were harassed and helpless, like sheep without a shepherd.

MATTHEW 9:35-36, RSV

Lord, thank you for my health. I suppose like most people I think about it most when I am sick. Then when I am strong again it seems like a miracle, so I thank you.

But lately, I have thought more about what health means when I am well, partly because I have heard that the world's number one health problem is one most people are either ignorant of or have no control over—malnutrition.

I am learning that this problem affects not only those who don't have enough to eat, but also those who eat too much—who are overnourished and therefore sometimes badly nourished.

So my growing awareness affects my life—physically as I pay more attention to what I eat, how active I am, and the drugs I take for granted; emotionally as I make decisions about schedules, life-style, and attitudes; spiritually as I am more thankful on a daily basis for the gift of health, and as I pray more regularly for innocent victims of malnutrition.

You came to minister to the *whole* person, and you never held back in responding to people's real needs whatever they were. You have always stood for the weak and the poor. Help me to stand with you. Make my purpose as yours—to make sure the poor have good news preached to them, in whatever form it takes.

67

VISIONS OF A WORLD HUNGRY

Remind me often that the poor are those who stand in need of you—and that includes me and all the rest of us in affluence who take our health for granted too often. Humble me to pray, by word and action, for the countless persons who suffer in obscurity because their plight lacks the drama to attract my attention and concern.

Lord, again, thank you for my health.
                                        Amen.

FOR FURTHER PRAYER AND ACTION

1. Have a thorough physical regularly.
2. Evaluate your current consumption of saturated fats, sugar, cholesterol, and refined foods. Seriously consider consuming more whole grains, potatoes, and other starchy foods, fresh fruits, and vegetables.
3. Engage in regular physical activity.
4. Consider eating less overall, thereby reducing competition between rich and poor for available food and agricultural resources.

❦ 12 ❦

HOPE

There is hope. I do not believe that the human race has inherited the genes of the dinosaur. I am convinced that humanity responds to the dream of beauty and peace, the dream of societies of persons whose physical needs for food, shelter, security and good health are assured, and which sings and dances in celebration of the accomplishment and maintenance of these dreams.[1]

C. DEAN FREUDENBERGER,
VISITING PROFESSOR *at School
of Theology at Claremont*

The better world to which idealists and dreamers have long aspired is no longer an unreachable dream. It is a real and practical possibility. For unquestionably, we do have the resources, the technological capability and the creative potential to do it. The only thing separating us from it is our moral and political will. And here man's highest moral and ethical insights reinforce the evidence of the physical world; concepts of brotherhood, caring and sharing should no longer be regarded as vague and pious ideals divorced from reality; they must now be seen as the indispensable prerequisite for the new set of realities on which the human future depends.[2]

MAURICE STRONG,
FORMER DIRECTOR
*United Nations Environment
Program*

VISIONS OF A WORLD HUNGRY

Brently Titcomb writes in a song sung by Anne Murray, "Lift your hearts and look to the sun, soon you'll see that we are one." John Denver says his dream of hope for a world hungry is expressed in his song "I Want to Live." It says in part, "We are standing on the threshold of a dream; no more hunger, no more war, no more wasting life away. It is simply an idea and I know its time has come."

Experts around the globe agree that technologically speaking we *can* end hunger and malnutrition, that it is not a pollyanna song, but a realizable goal within this century. Whether or not it is reached depends in part on how much this realistic hope is shared and acted upon by those who truly believe in the Hope of the world.

Jesus said to her, "I am the resurrection and the life; he who believes in me, though he die, yet shall he live, and whoever lives and believes in me shall never die. Do you believe this?"
JOHN 11:25-26, RSV

I rejoice in the Lord greatly that now at length you have revived your concern for me; you were indeed concerned for me, but you had no opportunity. Not that I complain of want; for I have learned, in whatever state I am, to be content. I know how to be abased, and I know how to abound; in any and all circumstances I have learned the secret of facing plenty and hunger, abundance and want. I can do all things in him who strengthens me.

Yet it was kind of you to share my trouble.
PHILIPPIANS 4:10-14, RSV

Truly, truly, I say to you, he who believes in me will also do the works that I do; and greater works than these will he do, because I go to the Father.
JOHN 14:12, RSV

70

HOPE

Lord, there are people who have curled up and died in a corner for no reason other than they lost hope. When there is no hope, there is no life. Without hope we give up—we lose our will to fight, to trust, to live.

There are too many people in this world today who have begun to lose hope—those who hunger for life's basic needs but see no relief; those who see too many problems and cannot find a solution.

When I begin to lose hope, too often I have forgotten that hope is inseparably connected to love and faith . . . your love which powerfully confirms that you are not only the bringer of life, but you *are* Life . . . faith that receives love humbly and enables me to respond with hope to even the most complicated problems.

Lord, the hunger problem seems hopeless to many, the victims and the bystanders. But hope needs opportunity, and just as Paul adapted to his situation in life, you have given me now an unparalleled chance to be a part of conquering this condition, conscious of your presence which supplies me with strength and with hope.

Together we as believers can never repay you for supplying our needs, but we can trust in the hope that you will continue to supply them through us and through all the means available today. Empowered by hope in you, we can do even greater works than you did on earth—if only we keep hope.

71

Lord, we do not hope in ourselves, our technology, our governments, our laws, our tenacity, our courage, or our will, though these things are all necessary to conquer hunger and provide justice. We hope in you. *Amen.*

and in your Son Jesus, who came to make your hope more real for us and who when he came taught us

FOR FURTHER PRAYER AND ACTION

to pray together: Our Father

1. Observe a special Sunday for hunger-related concerns.
2. If you belong to a prayer group, devote special time to praying for the hungry.
3. Obtain and distribute copies of your denomination's statements on hunger. If they do not have any, draft some and suggest their adoption.
4. Meditate on the biblical promise of hope in light of your response to the hunger/justice issue.

❧ 13 ❧

HUMAN DIGNITY

The whole future of food is linked to a very large group of complexities because . . . food is a very serious political problem, it is a very serious economic problem, and I would say it is a very serious moral problem.[1]

SARTAJ AZIZ, DEPUTY DIRECTOR,
World Food Council
United Nations

In these days of profound change, you will agree that dignity is probably the word that best describes the aspirations of an anxious humanity which refuses to give up all hope.

To half of mankind, however, to the people of the Third World, whose countries are periodically devastated by natural disasters, exploitation and war, dignity means, above all, a chance to work in peace for the development of their homelands and, more simply still, to escape at last from the degradation of famine and be able to provide for the most basic needs of their families.[2]

EDOUARD SAOUMA,
DIRECTOR-GENERAL
United Nations
Food and Agricultural
Organization

The development of peoples has the Church's close attention, particularly the development of those peoples who are striving to escape from hunger, misery, endemic diseases and

73

ignorance; of those who are looking for a wider share in the benefits of civilization and a more active improvement of their human qualities; of those who are aiming purposefully at their complete fulfillment.[3]

POPE PAUL VI

Put simply, the world is not just. At the root, the development of peoples in a way that insures human dignity is a moral problem. With the scientific and technological capabilities to provide the common good for all persons of (1) the right of access to the necessities of life, (2) self-determination, and (3) an environment which is renewable and sustainable, we are under judgment in our mission as Christians as to whether we will choose to do so.

Will we accept the mission to be the catalyst to bring about a sustainable global society that is governed by a new sort of science, technology, economics, and politics that maintains the community of all persons? Will we seek unity in communicating God's love in Christ for all persons? Will we participate in God's mission in the world to seek the common good for all persons and enhance the dignity, justice, and quality of their life as God meant it to be?

Blessed are the poor in spirit, for theirs is the kingdom of heaven.
Blessed are those who mourn, for they shall be comforted.
Blessed are the meek, for they shall inherit the earth.
Blessed are those who hunger and thirst for righteousness, for they shall be satisfied.
Blessed are the merciful, for they shall obtain mercy.
Blessed are the pure in heart, for they shall see God.
Blessed are the peacemakers, for they shall be called sons of God.

74

HUMAN DIGNITY

Blessed are those who are persecuted for righteousness'
sake, for theirs is the kingdom of heaven.
Blessed are you when men revile you and persecute you and
utter all kinds of evil against you falsely on my account.
Rejoice and be glad, for your reward is great in heaven,
for so men persecuted the prophets who were before you.

MATTHEW 5:3-12, RSV

Again Jesus spoke to them, saying, "I am the light of the
world; he who follows me will not walk in darkness, but will
have the light of life."

JOHN 8:12, RSV

This, then, is how you should pray:
"Our Father in heaven:
    May your holy name be honored;
    may your Kingdom come;
    may your will be done on
        earth as it is in heaven.
    Give us today the food we need.
    Forgive us the wrongs we have done,
        as we forgive the wrongs
            that others have done to us.
    Do not bring us to hard testing,
        but keep us safe from the Evil One."

MATTHEW 6:9-13, TEV

**Lord, your beatitudes are as paradoxical as
life—blessed and poor at the same time. And while
those in poverty are often thankful for small
blessings, I know you meant all those who recognize
their need of you. The poor are those who know what
justice, love, and human dignity are and can therefore
long for them.**

**Lord, open my ears to hear the cries for dignity from
an oppressed and sad humanity. Certainly dignity is**

not found in paternalism—in just giving the hungry
what they need for today over and over again.

It is found rather in the strength of affirmed
personhood which accepts everyone's freedom of
choice, in self-identity which gives people training and
tools to stand strong on their own, in a recognized full
humanity which includes a measure of divinity.

Help me be part of a church today that not only
laments a lack of justice, but creates a hunger and
thirst for it. Help me be a part of your revelation of
light to those in darkness.

Lord, so often I think I know mine and others' needs
as I pray for you to meet them. But you know our *real*
needs. If only we could live by the power of your
model prayer, and in meeting your needs, meet our
own as well. If we really sanctified your name, if we
really loved your kingdom, if we really did your will,
then our need for food, forgiveness, and protection
from temptation would be taken care of.

Thank you for meeting our needs even though we do
not meet yours. Help us distribute your abundance
fairly respecting the rights of all to share in what you
have provided. Thank you for endowing us with a
sense of worth and dignity. May we learn more of what
it means to share and practice that on earth.
                              Amen.

FOR FURTHER PRAYER AND ACTION

1. Treat people as persons, not functions such as "clerk," "station attendant," and so on.
2. Think about how you would feel if someone else always gave you food and clothing for your family.
3. Think about how you would feel if no one had confidence in your ability to learn to be self-sufficient.
4. Pray for the chronically unemployed and unemployable that they can maintain a sense of self-worth.

❧ 14 ❧

JUSTICE

There are four revolutionary and powerful elements which will affect the processes of change in the next decade. They are:
   —the demands of two-thirds of the earth's people
   —the ecological problems that threaten present and future generations
   —the misuse of power and the struggle of the powerless
   —the questioning of the growth-oriented affluent societies and the consequences of this for the rest of humankind.
Therefore there is urgent need to define new goals for both national and international societies.[1]

REPORT OF SECTION VI
HUMAN DEVELOPMENT:
AMBIGUITIES OF POWER,
TECHNOLOGY, AND QUALITY OF LIFE
Fifth Assembly of the World Council of Churches

I still have a dream today that one day justice will roll down like water, and righteousness like a mighty stream. I still have a dream today that in all of our state houses and city halls men will be elected to go there who will do justly and love mercy and walk humbly with their God.[2]

MARTIN LUTHER KING, JR.

The lessons of the nation's past tell us that liberty and justice cannot be secured for ourselves and kept from others without turning sour. Because we have cherished liberty for others, this country has sacrificed enormously (if not always wisely) in lives and material resources. We have not cherished justice as much. But justice and equality are no less a part of the nation's ideals, and we build on them by exercising them in our relationship with others. When we are rich and others are hungry or impoverished beyond description, justice calls for ending this imbalance.[3]

ARTHUR SIMON, DIRECTOR
Bread for the World

Hunger is the symptom. Lack of justice and human dignity is the real illness. At its root, the hunger/justice issue is a moral one.

There is no justice if rural people cannot make decisions for their own communities, if they are exploited by corporations, landowners, or politicians.

There is no justice if the land is abused and allowed to deteriorate so food cannot be grown.

There is no justice if farmers cannot get a fair price for what they produce.

There is no justice if there is no peace, where foreign or domestic troops are burning and plundering and there is no rural development.

There is no justice if the affluent consume a disproportionate share of the earth's resources by runaway consumerism.

For everything we read or see, we must ask: Is this just? For every issue and policy that is raised in our nation and in our community, we must ask: Is this just? How are hungry people affected?

The Lord is faithful in all his words,
and gracious in all his deeds.

VISIONS OF A WORLD HUNGRY

The Lord upholds all who are falling,
    and raises up all who are bowed down.
The eyes of all look to thee,
    and thou givest them their food
        in due season.
Thou openest thy hand,
    thou satisfiest the desire of every
        living thing.
The Lord is just in all his ways,
    and kind in all his doings.
The Lord is near to all who call upon him,
    to all who call upon him in truth.
He fulfils the desire of all who fear him,
    he also hears their cry, and saves them.
The Lord preserves all who love him;
    but all the wicked he will destroy.

                      PSALM 145:13b-20, RSV

I hate, I despise your feasts,
    and I take no delight in your
        solemn assemblies.
Even though you offer me your
        burnt offerings and cereal offerings,
    I will not accept them,
and the peace offerings of your fatted beasts
    I will not look upon.
Take away from me the noise of your songs;
    to the melody of your harps I will not listen.
But let justice roll down like waters,
    and righteousness like an everflowing stream.

                      AMOS 5:21-24, RSV

He has showed you, O man, what is good;
    and what does the Lord require of you
but to do justice, and to love kindness,
    and to walk humbly with your God?

                      MICAH 6:8, RSV

JUSTICE

Lord God, at the root of all these prayers and words about a world hungry is justice. I want a just world for my children, and I would say everyone else does also except that I see an abundance of injustice.

Today I share the dream of Micah and Martin Luther King, Jr., for justice. They knew that we are not likely to love you whom we have not seen unless we can come to love one another. They knew too that loving you leads to justice among us.

Measured by your justice, any nation would be overdeveloped whose standard of living was beyond the capacity of the world to generate for all its peoples. It is a revolutionary ethical concept, as is your gospel of love.

Because of that I can see that a just world involves a change in national goals and a restructuring of the international economic order. This takes time and a development of strategies to insure human dignity and purpose.

Lord, we have the resources and technological capacity to feed each person on this planet and more. The only thing separating us from that reality is our moral and political will. The concept of caring and sharing and the goal of justice should no longer be regarded as vague and pious ideals divorced from reality. They must now be seen as the indispensable reality on which the human future depends.

By our justice, or lack of it, we are choosing how long life on this planet will survive. O God, may we choose wisely.

Amen.

FOR FURTHER PRAYER AND ACTION

1. For every action of a school board, city council, public
   agency, or public official in your community, ask
   whether it is just.
2. What is the biblical view of justice? How does it differ
   from our legal definitions of justice?
3. How do you display justice, kindness, and humility in
   your life?
4. In the final analysis, does justice depend on any one
   type of political system? How can and does it exist in
   several?

❧ 15 ❧

KNOWLEDGE

Myth: Hunger and malnutrition are confined to a few remote places on earth.

Fact: Much of the world's population hasn't enough food or the right kinds of food.

Myth: All efforts are being made to increase food production.

Fact: Increased affluence means demand continues to outrun even increasing food supplies.

Myth: The tropics have plenty of rich, fertile soil for food production.

Fact: The lush green of tropical forests is most often a camouflage for impoverished soil.

Myth: Industrial pollution is primarily a city problem.

Fact: Evidence shows pollution affects climate in all parts of the world.

Myth: There are sufficient food reserves to protect us in emergencies.

Fact: Only four nations have significant food surplus, and very little is put on reserve against famine.

| Myth: | Machinery and chemicals will make growing food in the world easier. | Fact: | Petroleum for farm implements and agricultural chemicals is getting scarcer daily. |
| Myth: | We will always have food from the sea as a last resort. | Fact: | Oceans are being depleted of fish, and farming methods are difficult and expensive. |

The festival was nearly half over when Jesus went to the Temple and began teaching. The Jewish authorities were greatly surprised and said, "How does this man know so much when he has never been to school?"

Jesus answered, "What I teach is not my own teaching, but it comes from God, who sent me. Whoever is willing to do what God wants will know whether what I teach comes from God or whether I speak on my own authority. A person who speaks on his own authority is trying to gain glory for himself. But he who wants glory for the one who sent him is honest, and there is nothing false in him."

JOHN 7:14-18, TEV

You shall therefore lay up these words of mine in your heart and in your soul; and you shall bind them as a sign upon your hand, and they shall be as frontlets between your eyes. And you shall teach them to your children, talking of them when you are sitting in your house, and when you are walking by the way, and when you lie down, and when you rise. And you shall write them upon the doorposts of your house and upon your gates, that your days and the days of your children may be multiplied in the land which the Lord swore to your fathers to give them, as long as the heavens are above the earth.

DEUTERONOMY 11:18-21, RSV

KNOWLEDGE

And when Jesus had finished instructing his twelve disciples, he went on from there to teach and preach in their cities.
MATTHEW 11:1, RSV

Almighty and all-knowing God, I thank you that our
Lord has showed me how to use all of my heart and
soul and body and mind to love you. I thank you for
the gifts of intelligence and insight and the privilege
to grow in knowledge and understanding.

God, my knowledge about the world's poor and hungry
is still growing. There is widespread hunger in our
own nation and yet I do not always know who the poor
and hungry are in my own community or why they stay
that way. To respond at my best I need to know the
dimensions and causes of hunger, the process of
agricultural and rural development, and the biblical
and theological perspectives for the task. You have
called me to a sense of global responsibility for all
your children and to renew my commitment of
understanding and action in Christian love.

God, save me from pride, from believing only those
things which justify my present opinion, and from
discounting those things which require me to change.
Help me, rather, to see society as a whole, to find ways
to raise my awareness about the political, social,
cultural, and economic forces which cause people hurt,
and to keep current about the facts of the real world.

I know that the meaning of those facts depends on my
values and faith commitments as I interpret your call
to love and justice. May my partial knowledge be made
whole by your knowledge of me, and may I use that

85

knowledge to glorify you in a world where all your children live and move and have their being. In Jesus' name I pray.

Amen.

FOR FURTHER PRAYER AND ACTION

1. Learn the facts about the causes of world hunger.
2. Find out who is hungry in your neighborhood and why.
3. Read basic books about hunger.
4. Measure what you read against the biblical perspective of love and justice.
5. Help dispel myths about hunger in conversations with friends and acquaintances.

⚞ 16 ⚟

LIFE-STYLE

The attention given to saccharin, while almost nothing is said about the desperate need for a world food reserve program, shows how we occupy ourselves with trivial things and neglect what is essential.[1]

NORMAN E. BORLAUG,
GENETICIST
Nobel Prize Winner

The early monks practiced a simple life-style as an ascetic expression and symbol of their purity *from* the world. We can no longer afford that luxury. The practice of a simpler life-style on our part *in* the world is essential to the survival of human life.

Overconsumption and an affluent life-style (by any world standard) are among the prime causes of hunger and poverty, both in the United States and the world.

A simpler life-style is not a panacea. It may be embarked upon for the wrong reasons—out of guilt, as a substitute for political action, or in quest for moral "purity." But it can also be meaningful and significant:

—as an act of *faith* performed for the sake of personal integrity and as an expression of a personal commitment to a more equitable distribution of the world's wealth;

—as an act of *self-defense* against the mind-polluting effects of our overconsumption;

—as an act of *solidarity* with the majority of humankind, which has no choice about life-style;

—as an act of *celebration* of the riches found in creativity, spirituality, and community with others rather than in mindless materialism.

A recent Harris Survey revealed that 75 percent of American people polled said they are "willing to go without meat one day each week in order to send more food abroad to help nations with food shortages." Sixty-eight percent said they were prepared to "cut out all unessential uses of fertilizer here at home, including uses to beautify our lawns." This action could make more fertilizer available to others trying to grow food.

Adjusting to a life-style that is easier on the earth's resources, fairer in the light of the situation of the world's poor, and more beneficial to the physical, psychological, and moral health of the individual should not be all that painful—especially for the Christian who is willing to look at the world from Christ's perspective: the resources of the earth must be respected, conserved, and shared by all.

As Charles Birch has said, "The rich must live more simply that the poor may simply live."[2]

This is why I tell you: do not be worried about the food and drink you need in order to stay alive, or about clothes for your body. After all, isn't life worth more than food? And isn't the body worth more than clothes?

It is God who clothes the wild grass—grass that is here today and gone tomorrow, burned up in the oven. Won't he be all the more sure to clothe you? What little faith you have!

So do not start worrying: "Where will my food come from? or my drink? or my clothes?" (These are the things the pagans are always concerned about.) Your Father in heaven knows that you need all these things. Instead, be concerned above everything else with the Kingdom of God and with what he requires of you, and he will provide you with all these other things.

MATTHEW 6:25,30-33, TEV

You have heard that it was said, "You shall love your neighbor and hate your enemy." But I say to you, Love your enemies and pray for those who persecute you, so that you may be sons of your Father who is in heaven; for he makes his sun rise on the evil and on the good, and sends rain on the just and on the unjust.

MATTHEW 5:43-45, RSV

It was almost time for the Passover Festival, so Jesus went to Jerusalem. There in the Temple he found men selling cattle, sheep, and pigeons, and also the moneychangers sitting at their tables. So he made a whip from cords and drove all the animals out of the Temple, both the sheep and the cattle; he overturned the tables of the moneychangers and scattered their coins; and he ordered the men who sold the pigeons, "Take them out of here! Stop making my Father's house a marketplace!"

JOHN 2:13-16, TEV

Never eat more honey than you need; too much may make you vomit.

PROVERBS 25:16, TEV

Lord, I already know the best way to alter my life-style to the best advantage for all—live like Jesus. The Christian existence ideally is to imitate what you do. You send the sun and rain on everyone, you want me to get back to the basic facts of life, to love without reservation, to distinguish between life's needs and life itself, and seek first your kingdom knowing you will meet all my other needs.

Still it is easy to trust in the "things" of today and feel like it is up to me to see that humanity survives. Keep me from undue worry and pride. Remind me that life is a gift—not a right, and that my attitude toward the ultimate resources and values in life will determine how the earth's resources will be handled and provided for those who need them. I have already formed many habits of consuming and acting. Guide me in aligning my personal priorities to conform to my awareness of a world hungry. May my life-style become more compatible with our biosphere and supportive of peoples around the world.

Lord, help me choose a simpler life-style that promotes solidarity with the world's poor, helps me appreciate nature more, affords greater opportunity to work together with my neighbors, reduces my use of limited resources, creates greater inner harmony, saves money, allows time for meditation and prayer, incites me to take political and social action.

May all my decisions about my style of life celebrate the joy of life that comes from loving you.

Amen.

FOR FURTHER PRAYER AND ACTION

1. For *everything* you consume or purchase, ask whether it fulfills a personal want or a real need.
2. Next time you move, consider giving away items you haven't been using instead of trying to sell them.
3. Pray for guidance and strength to make changes in life-style that are difficult for you to consider.
4. Celebrate victories in life-style change.
5. Think through the steps in how a simpler life-style for you in a particular area actually helps the poor and hungry.

✎ 17 ✎

LOVE

I remember one time when I was a child of about five or six, my father had to go away for a business trip. So my mother, younger brother, and I went to visit my grandparents in Chicago. It was great fun to be there. Soon, however, I began to miss my father.

One day I noticed my mother writing a letter. "Can I write to Daddy, too?" I asked (I could not write at the time).

"Of course," came the reply, and soon I was trying my best to imitate the squiggly lines on the paper that I had seen my mother make. I told my father all about what I had been doing, where we had been, and how much I wished he'd hurry home. We put it in an envelope and sent it off.

A few days later Dad came to be with us. I remember the great excitement I felt when he arrived. He walked up to the front porch from the taxi carrying his suitcase. Still in his overcoat, he put down his bags, kissed my mother and began talking with the adults. I ran to the door from the other room where I had been watching out the window.

"Daddy, Daddy, did you get my letter?"

"Yes, Son, I sure did," he said as he picked me up in his arms. "Thank you very much."

"What did it say, Daddy? What'd it say?"

LOVE

He paused for a moment, looked at my mother, then back at me. "It said, 'I love you,'" came the thoughtful reply.

Imagine how much greater the love of God is. The gospel says that genuine love is evidenced by actual deeds not just empty words, that active love is based on experienced love.

How is love related to the hungry? How is it not?

Christian love means not only binding up wounds and being the good Samaritan after the event; it also has the duty of preventing wounds and thereby being effective in a deterrent way. Therefore, it will never merely accuse when confronted with misdeeds but will make effort to stop the source of the misdeeds. This means . . . that Christian love has a political dimension: it must also consider the social and economic structures in which one can live in peace and not be stimulated to hate, revenge, and disorder.[1]

HELMUT THIELICKE, PROFESSOR
OF SYSTEMATIC THEOLOGY
University of Hamburg

And the Word became flesh and dwelt among us, full of grace and truth; we have beheld his glory, glory as of the only Son from the Father.

JOHN 1:14, RSV

And one of the scribes came up and heard them disputing with one another, and seeing that he answered them well, asked him, "Which commandment is the first of all?" Jesus answered, "The first is, 'Hear, O Israel: The Lord our God, the Lord is one; and you shall love the Lord your God with all your heart, and with all your soul, and with all your mind, and with all your strength.' The second is this, 'You shall love your neighbor as yourself.' There is no other commandment greater than these."

MARK 12:28-31, RSV

This is how we know what love is: Christ gave his life for us. We too, then, ought to give our lives for our brothers! If a rich person sees his brother in need, yet closes his heart against his brother, how can he claim that he loves God? My children, our love should not be just words and talk; it must be true love, which shows itself in action.

What he commands is that we believe in his Son Jesus Christ and love one another, just as Christ commanded us. Whoever obeys God's commands lives in union with God and God lives in union with him. And because of the Spirit that God has given us we know that God lives in union with us.

1 JOHN 3:16-18, 23-24, TEV

How easy it is, Lord, to say, "Love one another," how hard to live. Sometimes when I look at that I think, Who was John trying to kid when he put that in his New Testament letter? Sometimes when I think about the way people mess up their lives or the helplessness of the poor and sick, loving begins to feel like a burden and an impossible task.

Yesterday I was reading about little Ben, a two-and-a-half-year-old boy who died of leukemia. I cried like a baby, especially as I thought about my little son Brian, and his tragic accident. One of the many things you have shown me about love is that the more I truly love the more vulnerable I am.

I guess that is why I am a little afraid or unsure about how to love a world hungry, until I remember that you did not ask me to love the world all at once, but the persons in it—like little Ben and Brian.

I have only got so much of that kind of love to spread around. So it will take a lot of us loving and deeply caring in specific ways to insure human decency and a

LOVE

full stomach for everyone. My love is finite but yours
is greater than the vastness of creation itself.

So I pray for strength in loving when it seems I cannot
any more, for forgiveness when I hold my love in, for
courage to risk love when I cannot see how I will be
loved back, for determination to translate my ideals
and attitudes of love into concrete action and
responsible citizenship.

In short, Lord, I wish I could love like you. Maybe the
more I practice it, the more I will be able to. Thanks
for loving me.

Amen.

FOR FURTHER PRAYER AND ACTION

1. Give gifts that reflect your global consciousness.
2. When dining out, order one meal for two and split it.
   Donate the extra money.
3. Share holiday meals with others.
4. Adopt a shut-in or other lonely person.
5. Verbalize and demonstrate your love for others, especially those who don't expect it.

❧ 18 ❧

MILITARISM

Every gun that is made, every warship launched, every rocket fired signifies, in the final sense, a theft from those who hunger and are not fed, those who are cold and not clothed.[1]

DWIGHT D. EISENHOWER

I offer you the choice of life or death, blessing or curse. Choose life and then you and your descendants will live.

DEUTERONOMY 30:19, NEB

So whatever you wish that men would do to you, do so to them; for this is the law and the prophets.

MATTHEW 7:12, RSV

If your enemy is hungry, feed him; if he is thirsty, give him a drink. You will make him burn with shame, and the Lord will reward you.

PROVERBS 25:21-22, TEV

He will settle disputes among great nations.
They will hammer their swords into plows
    and their spears into pruning knives.
Nations will never again go to war,
    never prepare for battle again.

ISAIAH 2:4, TEV

Annual cost for ending world illiteracy in five-year program.
(Estimate by UNICEF)
$1.6 billion[2]

Cost for solving the crisis of cities and human settlements.
(Estimate by environment expert Barbara Ward)
$25 billion

Annual cost for making "real impact" on the development crisis.
(Estimate by World Bank President Robert McNamara)
$15 billion

Annual cost for supplying everyone in the poor world with basic maternal health and family planning services.
(Estimate by food and population expert Lester Brown)
$2 billion

Annual cost for investment in land and water needed for poor nations to meet food production targets.
(Estimate by UN Food and Agricultural Organization)
$4.5 billion

Money needed now by poor countries to maintain essential imports.
(Estimate by World Bank, Washington)
$5.5 billion

ANNUAL WORLD EXPENDITURE ON ARMAMENTS　　**$200 billion***
(Estimate by United Nations)

TOTAL FOR ABOVE SERVICES TO THE WORLD FOR A YEAR　　**$53.6 billion†**

*Arthur Simon, Executive Director of Bread for the World, maintains that a more accurate figure for armaments would be $300 billion.
†All figures are in 1975 dollars.

VISIONS OF A WORLD HUNGRY

Lord, the world spends fifty times more for its militaries than it does for human development. It has been said that if only 10 percent of the world's military budgets were available, the global hunger problem could be solved. This nation spends seventy times more for military defense than for economic assistance. Why?

Our own history is filled with war after war, followed by various degrees of peace. In each war we seem to kill more than we thought possible. Our internal conflicts drive us more towards hate than love.

But, Lord, we feel trapped. So many of our jobs depend on defense. We feel responsible for freedom. We may be overtaken by our enemies if we let down.

Yet, we would like more peace than war, more life than death, more love than hate. we would like to trust and be trusted instead of greedily protecting what is "ours."

We would like to spend more on human need than on arms. It seems that our priorities should be more in the areas of education, job training, housing, and economic assistance to hungry nations than prestige, power, and profits.

Help us to dare to risk changing our priorities. Help us to trust in you that new ones can be built without national collapse. Help us to choose life in all its abundance.

Amen.

FOR FURTHER PRAYER AND ACTION

1. Pray for innocent victims of war and conflict and find out where they live.
2. Consider not buying consumer goods from companies that also manufacture arms.
3. Study military spending and its alternatives.
4. Protest the use of food as a weapon in our foreign policy.

✥ 19 ✥

MISSION

So many people still have the image of starving babies as the problem of hunger and our shipping food to some far-off land as the solution. There is so much more to it.

In today's church and world, we are in mission to each other. No longer is there such a clear distinction between the sender and receiver in mission. Together we seek the common good for all persons.

Over the past six years my church has developed strong friendships with some people in Tecate, Mexico, through our work with the Methodist church there. Our friends are poor. Most live in shacks with dirt floors. Running water and toilets are rare. When they dress up they wear the best of what we have discarded. Most families have no visible means of support.

Last fall a group of them came to visit us for a Sunday service and picnic afterwards. My family ate with the Reverend Verdusco, Javier (a teenager), and two elderly women. Javier has had two years of English and hopes someday to be a doctor. Why? "Because so many people are sick," he says.

The Reverend Verdusco's own baby was home with a high fever. If it persisted until Monday he would travel the thirty miles to Tijuana for help. Neither was the baby well who came with our visitors that Sunday. The baby was held for a while by a large white-haired woman al-

most blind from cataracts, which would have been re-
moved by now had she lived in this country.

The woman next to me remarked on my son's blond hair
(she has seen few Anglos). She has no grandchildren because her only son is not married.

The other woman told me she had ten children. Not all
had lived because, as she motioned and spoke in Spanish,
they had not had enough to eat.

It was her hard and callous hands I held in the circle of
song and prayer as we closed our visit together that afternoon. As they all prayed out loud in Spanish for us,
they sang a song where everyone greets one another by
shaking hands and then embracing. Singing and smiling
they made their way to each one of us as we all embraced
each and every person.

And that is what they are saying—each and every person is worthy of being embraced and each one *is* embraced by our one Lord. That is how and why we work
together in mission, teaching each other. That is how and
why we work for human dignity. And human dignity is the
real issue in the hunger/justice problem. The solution is
linked to whether our prayers of love will turn into acts of
embracing the real needs of real people.

Now in these days prophets came down from Jerusalem to
Antioch. And one of them named Agabus stood up and foretold
by the Spirit that there would be a great famine over all the
world; and this took place in the days of Claudius. And the
disciples determined, every one according to his ability, to
send relief to the brethren who lived in Judea; and they did so,
sending it to the elders by the hand of Barnabas and Saul.

ACTS 11:27-30, RSV

Go therefore and make disciples of all nations, baptizing
them in the name of the Father and of the Son and of the Holy

Spirit, teaching them to observe all that I have commanded you; and lo, I am with you always, to the close of the age.

MATTHEW 28:19-20, RSV

Our Savior wants everyone to be saved and to come to know the truth.

1 TIMOTHY 2:4, TEV

God, Creator and Author of Life, warned anew of the threats to human survival, we confess that the way we live and order society sets us against one another and alienates us from your creation, exploiting as though dead, things to which you have given life. Separated from you we live in emptiness. We long in our own lives for a new spirituality of intention, thought, and action. Help us to struggle to conserve the earth for future generations, and free us to share together, that all may be free.

KYRIE ELEISON
(Lord have mercy)

God of love, who through Jesus Christ shares our suffering, forgives our sins, and delivers from the bondage of oppression, help us to desire and nourish in ourselves sustaining community with our brothers and sisters everywhere. Give us courage to share suffering when it comes. Restore to us the joy of Resurrection, that in the midst of situations we can hardly bear we may sing out:

HALLELUJAH
(Praise be to you, O Lord)

God of hope, whose spirit gives light and power to your people, empower us to witness to your name in all the nations, to struggle for your own justice

against all principalities and powers and to persevere with faith and humor in the tasks that you have given to us. Without you we are powerless. Therefore we cry together:

MARANATHA
(Come, Lord Jesus)

And grant that we may with one voice and one heart glorify and sing praise to the majesty of your holy name, of the Father, the Son, and the Holy Spirit.*

Amen.

FOR FURTHER PRAYER AND ACTION

1. Sponsor a hunger field trip for youth.
2. Ask for a task force on hunger to be formed in your church. If there already is one, join it.
3. Invite foreign students, missionaries, or others from developing countries to speak at your church.
4. Visit at least one place of your denomination's United States mission on your next vacation.

*Closing prayer of the Fifth Assembly of the World Council of Churches meeting in Nairobi, Kenya, December 1975. The largest ecumenical gathering of Christians ever assembled in the history of the church.

❦ 20 ❧

POPULATION

For the great majority of countries, a doubling of populations will yield potentially unmanageable ecological, economic,
and political stresses.[1]

LESTER BROWN, PRESIDENT
Worldwatch Institute

Poverty means population rates stay high.

**According to India's former Minister of State for Fam-
ily Planning, hunger induces women in his country to
produce from eight to ten children on the assumption that
only three will live to become breadwinners.**

**Most poor families will not start having fewer children
until their standard of living and health improves and
they feel secure enough to realize that it is in their own
economic interest to do so. United Nations demographers
support this by noting lower birthrates in countries
where standards rise.**

**Even so, population growth is outdistancing food pro-
duction, and the two must be brought into balance. This
won't happen, however, until the hungry nations can
grow their own food.**

**Population control is essential, but the vital strategy
for controlling populations is seeing to it that people now
living on the earth can feed themselves.**

Governments are faced with only one real choice—not

104

whether population growth will slow, but how. Will birth rates fall as human needs are met, or will death rates continue to increase, as they have over the last five years, as food producing systems deteriorate and food scarcities become even more serious?

Then God said, "Let us make man in our image, after our likeness; and let them have dominion over the fish of the sea, and over the birds of the air, and over the cattle, and over all the earth, and over every creeping thing that creeps upon the earth." So God created man in his own image, in the image of God he created him; male and female he created them. And God blessed them, and God said to them, "Be fruitful and multiply, and fill the earth and subdue it; and have dominion over the fish of the sea and over the birds of the air and over every living thing that moves upon the earth."

GENESIS 1:26-28, RSV

The kind of fasting I want is this: Remove the chains of oppression and the yoke of injustice, and let the oppressed go free. Share your food with the hungry and open your homes to the homeless poor. Give clothes to those who have nothing to wear, and do not refuse to help your own relatives.

ISAIAH 58:6-7, TEV

For God so loved the world that he gave his only Son, that whoever believes in him should not perish but have eternal life. For God sent the Son into the world, not to condemn the world, but that the world might be saved through him.

JOHN 3:16-17, RSV

The year 2000. Four, eight, twelve billion people. People, people, and more people. God, it seems incredible to me that nobody planned for this. Twice as many people crowding the same space in my

lifetime. Three times as many in the lifetime of my children.

An image of a sea of faces, mostly children without homes, hungry, pitiful. More mouths to feed, more jobs to create, more homes to build, more people to relate to, more competition, more mental illness, more drug addiction.

Why? I can pretend it won't affect me, and that life will be just the same in twenty years as it is now. I can go on living as if those unborn children are just numbers and the problems of other nations. But I know they are not. We all have enough trouble coping now. What will it be like then? There is enough self-centeredness and power-mania now. What will it be like then when more people want the same things? If you could mastermind creation, why couldn't you let us know about this? I guess you did.

We heard about the population explosion a few years back, but found it hard to believe. Now we know that people keep multiplying in part because of their tragic circumstances in life. What they are really fighting for is the right to live, to realize the potential they were born with.

Some advocate that we simply have to let people starve to death in societies that fail to cut their birth rates. To me that is morally repulsive. And the moral question of the quality of life is one I cannot ignore any longer and still claim to be yours. Help me respond to the real issues, and may your grace guide us all.

Amen.

106

FOR FURTHER PRAYER AND ACTION

1. Make a hunger map showing where hungry people live.
2. Participate in community and school efforts to make birth control information available to all who need it, including youth.
3. Ask your Congress-person to support policies giving aid to the most needy nations, not just those to whom it is politically expedient.
4. Remember that *all* persons born on this planet have the right to life.

❧ 21 ❧

POVERTY

Senator Ernest F. Hollings of South Carolina is a concerned Christian who once believed that the poor could climb to prosperity if they just tried.

I was a victim of hunger myopia. I didn't really see hunger until I visited some families in a Charleston, South Carolina slum. Before we had gone a block I was miserable. I began to understand that hunger is real, that it exists in hundreds of humans in my own home city. I saw what all America needs to see. The hungry are not able-bodied men, sitting around drunk and lazy on welfare. They are children. They are abandoned women, or the crippled, or the aged. This country, with its great wealth and energy, has the ability to wipe out hunger almost overnight. We can, we just haven't.[1]

The major crises of our times are not unrelated accidents, mere coincidental aberrations from an otherwise well-regulated world system.

The problems of food, population, employment and environment are now recognized as symptoms of the same sickness. And it is clear that a cure will not be found without a diagnosis of what that sickness is.

Recent events have made it blazingly clear that this single global crisis, the sickness which underlies the symptoms, is none other than common poverty compounded by chronic inequality.[2]

PETER ADAMSON
New Internationalist

POVERTY

69% of *all* poor, by governmental figures, are white . . . But
10% of all whites are poor
33.9% of all Blacks are poor
24.3% of all Spanish speaking are poor,
40-50% of all Native Americans are poor.[3]

> POVERTY PROFILE,
> *Campaign for Human
> Development, U. S. Catholic
> Conference* (1972)

According to figures released by the Population Reference Bureau, the World Bank Group, and the United Nations, there is a startling gap between the rich and the poor:

Country	Per Capita GNP ($)	Life Expectancy	Infant Mortality/1,000	Percentage Literacy
Niger	90	38	169	9
India	110	50	139	28
Sri Lanka	110	68	177	5
Nigeria	130	41	180	25
Egypt	240	52	103	30
Japan	2,320	73	12	98
Sweden	4,480	71	10	99
U. S.	5,590	71	18	98

When you harvest your fields, do not cut the grain at the edges of the fields, and do not go back to cut the heads of grain that were left. Do not go back through your vineyard to gather the grapes that were missed or to pick up the grapes that have fallen; leave them for poor people and foreigners. I am the Lord your God.

LEVITICUS 19:9-10, TEV

If there is among you a poor man, one of your brethren, in any of your towns within your land which the Lord your God gives you, you shall not harden your heart or shut your hand against your poor brother, but you shall open your hand to him, and lend him sufficient for his need, whatever it may be. You shall give to him freely, and your heart shall not be grudging when you give to him; because for this the Lord your God will bless you in all your work and in all that you undertake. For the poor will never cease out of the land; therefore I command you, You shall open wide your hand to your brother, to the needy and to the poor, in the land.

DEUTERONOMY 15:7-8,10-11, RSV

The Spirit of the Lord is upon me,
because he has anointed me to preach good news to the poor.
He has sent me to proclaim release to the captives
and recovering of sight to the blind,
to set at liberty those who are oppressed,
to proclaim the acceptable year of the Lord.

LUKE 4:18-19, RSV

"To each according to his need" is an idea that was around long before Marx and Engels. I read in the Bible, Lord, that over and over you made provisions for the weak and poor in the law. Government institutions were to insure the poor's welfare, and everyone was to demonstrate a deep concern for individuals in the community. It also says that if your will was completely fulfilled, there would have been no poor and no debts.

But you, Lord, made these laws because you knew your will would not be done. Unfortunately, it seems that times have changed little. *Poor* is still a relative word, but today the gap between the rich and poor is growing, and instead of freedom being used to fulfill the community welfare, it becomes a license to accumulate and hoard in the name of hard work and the right to take what you can get.

110

POVERTY

Today, as in ancient times, the sickness of affluence is
its poverty and inequality. And the worst part is that we
acknowledge our need for shame by keeping the disease
hidden instead of confessing our greed and meeting it
head on. The disease of poverty afflicts more than forty
million in the United States alone, and more than
two-thirds of the entire world.

Lord, I am ashamed since I know I am responsible. I
have been lucky never to have lived in real poverty. Yet
you have shown me the sad and empty faces of those
who do, and I have wept in anger and despair. I pray
that your spirit would also come upon me and on all who
are too comfortable in the church.

Convict us with a new sense of urgency to do more than
pity and pray for the poor. Help us to see that poverty is
a symptom of our lack of vision and hardness of heart.
Help us not complacently accept it as a necessary
side effect of our wealth.

May we be willing to risk providing even the rudiments
of decency for those who simply want to enjoy being
alive. May we be willing to sacrifice and change for the
sake of our sisters and brothers in need wherever they
live in this world. And in doing so, may we live with the
assurance and confidence that this is indeed good news.
Amen.

FOR FURTHER PRAYER AND ACTION

1. Grow a garden and give away the food to the needy in your community.
2. Try living on a poverty budget for a week.
3. Find out if the children of needy families in your area participate in federal programs which provide a hot breakfast and lunch.
4. Be aware of the prejudice in our society against those who are poor. Pray for strength not to participate in it yourself.

~ 22 ~

RACISM

We had just finished playing miniature golf. It had been my four-year-old daughter Chris's request for an outing, and I enjoyed being alone with her having fun. We played at the newest extravaganza miniature golf place in town, complete with castle, running water, dragons, and lots of other fairyland-type structures. The course itself was boring, but Chris thought it was heaven!

She had to go to the bathroom now so we found our way through the huge arcade building to the back. Afterward she wanted to play a machine. All I had left was one quarter so we began to look around for the best one, she looking for one she could make move herself, I looking for something mild. Guns, tanks, bombs plus a lot of noise didn't help us choose.

Finally I found one that looked like a simple motorcycle drive. It was a TV with a road going back and forth across the screen. The handlebars controlled a little man and motorcycle. Easy I thought, keep the man on the road. I told Chris how to do it. Sounded fine to her, but she wanted me to hold the handlebars with her since they were too hard for her small hands to turn alone. I agreed. In went the quarter.

The road began to move and we moved our man, keeping him centered on the road. All of a sudden another man and motorcycle zoomed past us on the screen. We swerved to miss him. Must be a race I thought. Chris seemed to be having fun.

Another man approached fast. Then ... BAM!! We hit him! I thought a gun had gone off. The machine jolted with the loud noise and the TV screen lit up with flashing lights like a bomb had exploded! As fast as it happened, it stopped. Our man was still on the road. I was visibly shaken, my heart pounding. Chris was silent—almost stunned.

"We hit him!" I said, trying to make light of it. "We'd better be more careful." I did try hard to avoid having it happen again, but it was impossible. Again and again we kept hitting them.

When the machine stopped, I took her hand and, ignoring our score, we walked outside to the car. After a moment I asked her if she liked playing miniature golf, but it was hard for both of us to remember the feeling we had had playing.

On the way home we talked more about the day and playing golf. We'd had a great time. Then after some silence Chris said, "Daddy, I didn't like that motorcycle game. When we hit that man we couldn't even stop to see if he was hurt!"

Among segments of the U.S. population that experience hunger disproportionately, federal statistics point especially to native Americans. They suffer the most malnutrition, the most illness, the highest infant mortality rate and the lowest life expectancy of any group in the United States. This tragic situation has to be one of the ironies of the nation's history.[1]

ARTHUR SIMON, DIRECTOR,
Bread for the World

"Who is my neighbor?"

Jesus answered, "There was once a man who was going

down from Jerusalem to Jericho when robbers attacked him, stripped him, and beat him up, leaving him half dead. It so happened that a priest was going down that road; but when he saw the man, he walked on by on the other side. In the same way a Levite also came there, went over and looked at the man, and then walked on by on the other side. But a Samaritan who was traveling that way came upon the man, and when he saw him, his heart was filled with pity. He went over to him, poured oil and wine on his wounds and bandaged them; then he put the man on his own animal and took him to an inn, where he took care of him. The next day he took out two silver coins and gave them to the innkeeper. 'Take care of him,' he told the innkeeper, ' and when I come back this way, I will pay you whatever else you spend on him.'"

And Jesus concluded, "In your opinion, which one of these three acted like a neighbor toward the man attacked by the robbers?"

The teacher of the Law answered, "The one who was kind to him."

Jesus replied, "You go, then, and do the same."

LUKE 10:29b-37, TEV

Jesus said, "I came to this world to judge, so that the blind should see and those who see should become blind."

Some Pharisees who were there with him heard him say this and asked him, "Surely you don't mean that we are blind, too?"

Jesus answered, "If you were blind, then you would not be guilty; but since you claim that you can see, this means that you are still guilty."

JOHN 9:39-41, TEV

Lord, it is unfair that blacks and poor persons go to jail more often than whites with money and receive harder sentences than whites convicted of the same crime.

115

It is unfair that native Americans receive the lowest
annual family income of all ethnic groups in the
United States and that their infant mortality rate is
22.4 percent higher than the national average.

Racism! If a record could be compiled of all that has
happened between the races, it would make an
enormous book which the reader would have to turn
over unread because its contents would be too horrible.

Lord, I confess that I am part of the problem of
racism. I give thanks that, because of your divine love
within me, I am also part of the solution. You have
shown me that love must know no limits of race, that
my neighbor is whoever needs me, and whoever at any
given time and place I can help with my active love.

I pray for myself and all those who claim to stand with
you, that we face our racism. Let us recognize even
symbolic racism which protests welfare, militance,
crime, fair housing, and affirmative action programs
as a cover for the inner conflict we feel about race. Let
us not be content either with reverse discrimination
and teaching our children that quotas and
measurement of ethnic background, while necessary
temporarily, are an adequate response to the more
fundamental question of human value.

I pray for the church as it deals with this issue and its
relationship to the rights of all people to the basic
necessities of life. May we become a model of a
nonracist community. May we actively involve
members of minority and racially oppressed groups in
the decision-making process of the church. May we

stand firm against apartheid and actively initiate
campaigns to support the struggle against it. May we
not be afraid to confront institutional racism that
maintains the affluent world's privilege at the expense
of a hungry one.

Lord, help me to identify with the feelings of anger,
defeat, and defiance that permeate the lives of
persons victimized by racist actions and policies. Help
me to channel my indignation in constructive, loving,
and forgiving ways. Help me grow in your spirit.
Amen.

FOR FURTHER PRAYER AND ACTION

1. Invite foreign visitors into your home.
2. Celebrate and affirm your ethnic heritage.
3. Be aware of how subtle racism denies human rights.
   Stand with the victims of racist decisions and policies.
4. Meditate seriously about all your feelings toward persons of differing racial background, whether near or far geographically. Measure them against agape love.

≈ 23 ≈

RESPONSIBILITY

The existing order is coming apart, and rightly so, since it has failed to meet the needs of the vast majority of peoples and reserved its benefits for a privileged minority. The task is to create another one.

DAG HAMMARSKJÖLD
Report, 1975

The stark realities of the world food crisis have suddenly made hunger a priority item on the agenda of the American churches. For years there have been many voices predicting the coming of this crisis, but it is only the beginning of extensive famine and starvation . . . that . . . the American public and the American churches have begun to take notice. . . .

It is tragic that millions will die in order to capture the attention of the more prosperous peoples of the world. It will be doubly tragic if the response of the Church remains at the superficial level of self-righteous charity. The danger is that a local congregation may fast, contribute money and study hunger during Lent and then feel it has discharged its obligation of concern. . . . The meaning of the Church as the people of God is more intimately tied up with the welfare of the hungry, the poor, the needy and the oppressed than this.[1]

BRUCE BIRCH,
PROFESSOR OF OLD TESTAMENT
Wesley Theological Seminary

The relations of the global food crisis and the religious community in the United States is so compelling that it requires continuing prayerful reflection and public reiteration.

118

RESPONSIBILITY

Our response to the problem must be proportional to its scope and seriousness. Hunger today . . . cannot be adequately confronted as an issue for private or personal charity alone. The need is for a response at the level of public policy, nationally and internationally. As the largest food producing and exporting nation in the world, our policy is critically important. The first contribution the religious communities can make is to build a community of conscience in the country supporting a U.S. food policy which meets the demands of national and international justice.

DR. CLAIRE RANDALL,
GENERAL SECRETARY OF THE
NATIONAL COUNCIL OF
CHURCHES;
BISHOP JAMES RAUSCH,
GENERAL SECRETARY OF THE
U.S. CATHOLIC CONFERENCE;
RABBI HENRY SEIGMAN,
PRESIDENT OF THE
SYNAGOGUE
COUNCIL OF AMERICA

People ask, "How can I respond?" The answer is to begin where you are. Take simple steps first. Set expectations you can meet. Make your response a matter of daily prayer. Respond not out of a sense of guilt but because of the gospel imperative of love and justice and God's affirmation of life.

The hunger issue can be a negative and depressing one if we let it. Take the positive approach. Respond because there is hope and because God gives us the strength to be a part of it.

God gives you the task. He does not ask that you succeed, but he does ask that you not lay it aside.

JEWISH PROVERB

119

VISIONS OF A WORLD HUNGRY

But be doers of the word, and not hearers only, deceiving yourselves.

JAMES 1:22, RSV

When the Son of Man comes as King and all the angels with him, he will sit on his royal throne, and the people of all the nations will be gathered before him. Then he will divide them into two groups, just as a shepherd separates the sheep from the goats. He will put the righteous people at his right and the others at his left. Then the King will say to the people on his right, "Come, you that are blessed by my Father! Come and possess the kingdom which has been prepared for you ever since the creation of the world. I was hungry and you fed me, thirsty and you gave me a drink; I was a stranger and you received me in your homes, naked and you clothed me; I was sick and you took care of me, in prison and you visited me." The righteous will then answer him, "When, Lord, did we ever see you hungry and feed you, or thirsty and give you a drink? When did we ever see you a stranger and welcome you in our homes, or naked and clothe you? When did we ever see you sick or in prison, and visit you?" The King will reply, "I tell you, whenever you did this for one of the least important of these brothers of mine, you did it for me!"

MATTHEW 25:31-40, TEV

You are the light of the world. A city set on a hill cannot be hid. Nor do men light a lamp and put it under a bushel, but on a stand, and it gives light to all in the house. Let your light so shine before men, that they may see your good works and give glory to your Father who is in heaven.

MATTHEW 5:14-16, RSV

You call me Teacher and Lord; and you are right, for so I am. If I then, your Lord and Teacher, have washed your feet, you also ought to wash one another's feet.

JOHN 13:13-14, RSV

120

RESPONSIBILITY

And he sat down and called the twelve; and he said to them, "If any one would be first, he must be last of all and servant of all."

MARK 9:35, RSV

Make the Shakertown Pledge your prayer of commitment. It originated when a group of religious retreat-center directors gathered at the site of a restored Shaker village near Harrodsburg, Kentucky, and were moved to covenant in response to the poverty crisis.

THE SHAKERTOWN PLEDGE

Recognizing that the earth and the fulness thereof is a gift from our gracious God, and that we are called to cherish, nurture, and provide loving stewardship for the earth's resources,

And recognizing that life itself is a gift, and a call to responsibility, joy, and celebration, I make the following declarations:

1. I declare myself to be a world citizen.
2. I commit myself to lead an ecologically sound life.
3. I commit myself to lead a life of creative simplicity and to share my personal wealth with the world's poor.
4. I commit myself to join with others in reshaping institutions in order to bring about a more just global society in which each person has full access to the needed resources for their physical, emotional, intellectual, and spiritual growth.
5. I commit myself to occupational accountability, and in so doing I will seek to avoid the creation of products which cause harm to others.
6. I affirm the gift of my body, and commit myself to its proper nourishment and physical well-being.

121

7. I commit myself to examine continually my relations with others, and to attempt to relate honestly, morally, and lovingly to those around me.
8. I commit myself to personal renewal through prayer, meditation and study.
9. I commit myself to responsible participation in a community of faith.

FOR FURTHER PRAYER AND ACTION

1. Ask for food donations at stores and distribute them to those in need.
2. Educate people about hunger at public dinners with posters and placemats that display the issue.
3. Volunteer for Meals on Wheels, FISH, or other community food and help programs.
4. Have more than one church dinner a year on this issue. To vary the format, pick and follow a theme from this book that relates to hunger.

~ 24 ~

RURAL LEADERSHIP

One very serious cause of hunger is the dearth of rural and agricultural leadership. In the former colonies personnel were trained for government, industry, and for the production of nonfood producing agricultural industries. The agricultural leaders that did get training received it in temperate zone methods, often inappropriate for the different soils and climates of the tropics where most of the world's hungry people live.

This, combined with the low status in developing countries of most agricultural leaders (including low salaries) and other social and psychological factors, has brought us to a point where there are not enough rural leaders.

Sometimes there is interference with a genuine dedication to solving the rural problems because of the deceiving attraction of city life. Famine drives the rural population to the cities in search of a better life, but unlike Europe at the beginning of the industrial revolution, there is no industry requiring their unskilled hands. And so slums begin to weaken economic and leadership growth.

Today, every farmer is entitled to sufficient technical knowledge about planting and breeding. Money needs to be put into agricultural research in the heavily populated tropics, and the results must reach *every* farmer. Leadership must be found and trained to teach tropic zone agriculture.

The churches are in a favorable position to respond. We have a long history of scholarship programs for leadership training, both here and abroad. Our history of priority on training strong church leaders in every nation is paying off. Seventy to 80 percent of all leaders in Africa today received their education through the church. We have a worldwide network for training potential rural leaders. We are already starting to support more tropic zone research in our own country.

Our task is before us. The outcome means being that much closer to seeing people freed from hunger.

Moses heard all the people complaining as they stood around in groups at the entrances of their tents. He was distressed because the Lord had become angry with them, and he said to the Lord, "Why have you treated me so badly? Why are you displeased with me? Why have you given me the responsibility for all these people? I didn't create them or bring them to birth! Why should you ask me to act like a nurse and carry them in my arms like babies all the way to the land you promised to their ancestors? Where could I get enough meat for all these people? They keep whining and asking for meat. I can't be responsible for all these people by myself; it's too much for me! If you are going to treat me like this, have pity on me and kill me, so that I won't have to endure your cruelty any longer."

The Lord said to Moses, "Assemble seventy respected men who are recognized as leaders of the people, bring them to me at the Tent of my presence, and tell them to stand there beside you. I will come down and speak with you there, and I will take some of the spirit I have given you and give it to them. Then they can help you bear the responsibility for these people, and you will not have to bear it alone."

NUMBERS 11:10-17, TEV

RURAL LEADERSHIP

Lord, the saying of Jesus that a prophet has no
honor in his own country surely seems true on
many fronts. Certainly in the area of rural leadership
hungry nations have long sought solutions to food
production and development from sources outside
their borders.

I am not a farmer, but it does not take long for anyone
who is interested to find out that tragically this help
has not provided for long-term self-sufficiency in food
that would stem chronic hunger. The World Food
Council goals reinforce and facilitate a process of
responsible rural leadership and development.

God, may we in the institutional church see the
encouragement of our government to actively support
these goals as part of our moral obligation and
response to the hungry.

Certainly they need
- an early warning system to foretell changes in the
  food situation worldwide
- an international food reserve to stave off inevitable
  years of bad harvest or disaster
- a multimillion-dollar agricultural fund
- a regulation of the use of the ocean
- an end to the arms race.

No one can do it alone, and as Moses felt his burden
relieved in sharing it with others, may we too
recognize that our service to you cannot be ultimately
done without your aid, and that your work cannot be
accomplished fully without us.

Therefore, help us not only to do our part in sharing the responsibility for feeding the world, but help us actively train and prepare others in this pursuit.

Amen.

FOR FURTHER PRAYER AND ACTION

1. Support exchange students in rural development. Make sure they attend a school that teaches appropriate technology for their home situation.
2. Encourage local agricultural students to become educated about farming techniques needed in growing regions of the world outside the United States.
3. Find out which development projects your denomination supports which provide rural leadership training. Promote them.
4. Visit a farm to find out what it really takes to produce food on a large scale.

～ 25 ～

SELF-DETERMINATION

Two magazines arrived in the same day's mail. One was the *New Internationalist* with a special article on Southern Africa. The other was *U. S. News and World Report* with an ad paid for by the Consul (commercial) South African Consulate General. They offered interesting comparisons:

N.I.—"The blacks in South Africa have an average income of $160 a year . . . and South Africa is the richest nation on the African continent. There is no excuse for the malnutrition, disease and illiteracy and poverty which afflict so many of its people."

U.S. News—"Maybe you've been buying or investing abroad but getting less than you bargained for. We'll restore your faith . . . We'll give you an idea what you've been missing in South Africa. It's not just what you do, it's where you do it. So, the next time, think South Africa. It's better for your business."

N.I.—"In the grand design for my homeland, I see many white capitalists making vast amounts of money." Professor Ntsanwist, Chief Minister of Gazankula.

U.S. News—"An agricultural bounty that includes some of the best wines, canned, dried and fresh fruits and fish products, as well as wool, hides, sugar, corn and much more."

N.I.—"Apartheid is not racism for its own sake—it is an economic system which shows no signs of changing. As Prime Minister Vorster said on 24th April 1968, 'It is true that there are Blacks working for us. They will continue to work for us for generations, in spite of the ideal that we have to separate them completely. . . . But the fact that they work for us can never entitle them to claim political rights. Not now, nor in the future . . . under no circumstances.'"

U.S. News—"We've got a climate for profitable enterprise that makes you feel right at home."

The Christian response to this is symbolized by a bumper sticker I saw recently. It said,

Jesus is coming . . .
And is he gonna be mad!

All over the world people are becoming more determined than ever to participate in decision making, in efforts toward self-reliance, in movements of various kinds which give them scope to be themselves and to be authentically with others. They no longer accept passive roles, or being treated as objects rather than subjects. Even the pundits of science and technology now realize that such matters as nuclear energy, genetics, and planning can no more be left to governments and other power elites. The people themselves should be allowed to see the issues and express themselves on options.[1]

PHILIP POTTER,
GENERAL SECRETARY
World Council of Churches

The Lord has taken his place to contend,
    he stands to judge his people.
The Lord enters into judgment
    with the elders and princes of his people.
"It is you who have devoured the vineyard,
    the spoil of the poor is in your houses.
What do you mean by crushing my people,
    by grinding the face of the poor?"
        says the Lord God of hosts.
ISAIAH 3:13-15, RSV

SELF-DETERMINATION

Come, all who are thirsty, come, fetch water;
come, you who have no food, buy corn and eat;
come and buy, not for money, not for a price.
Why spend money and get what is not bread,
    why give the price of your labour and go unsatisfied?
Only listen to me and you will have good food to eat,
    and you will enjoy the fat of the land.
Come to me and listen to my words,
    hear me, and you shall have life.

ISAIAH 55:1-3a, NEB

You yourselves are the letter we have, written on our hearts
for everyone to know and read. It is clear that Christ himself
wrote this letter and sent it by us. It is written, not with ink
but with the Spirit of the living God, and not on stone tablets
but on human hearts.

2 CORINTHIANS 3:2-3, TEV

**Lord, I pray for more understanding and appreciation
for the complexities of development. There is still
such a debate going on and it seems to boil down again
to the haves and the have nots.**

**I pray for the vision of a prophet like Isaiah who was
able to tear away the veil of custom and appearance
and address the real situation.**

**I pray that my government and other affluent nations
would not continue to force their concepts of
development on others, or promote the status quo.**

**So often we have seen that economic growth by itself,
in hopes that the benefits will "trickle down" to the
poor and needy, has been a mistake and a lie which
has not insured development with integrity. It has
benefited the few at the expense of the many.**

129

It is obvious that development continues, but on whose terms? And why is poverty and inequality increasing in its wake? As the world's richest nation, may our influence on the development of peoples focus on *human* development.

May we work to enhance peoples' economic needs now, not just promise them in some distant future. May our assistance not just be to the affluent and privileged minority in developing countries who are already overdeveloped in comparison to the poverty and misery of the poor.

May our policies of aid, education, and technology enable people to be an effective part of the development process, so that they may utilize their skills and potentials and receive a return for their contribution to production.

Lord, I pray for extension workers, agronomists, biologists, medical and technical advisors, and others in developing countries as they relate to individual people. Help them build trusting relationships from which a new sense of purpose, pride, and honor can be generated.

May all people be allowed to exercise their potential and freedom of choice in determining their own life and livelihood.

Amen.

SELF-DETERMINATION

FOR FURTHER PRAYER AND ACTION

1. How does your education relate to your independence?
2. Support mission development projects which allow participants to decide the direction of the work.
3. Support the right of the poor to organize for fair wages and decent working conditions.
4. Pray for the victims of apartheid.

❦ 26 ❧

STEWARDSHIP

I do not want to be a member of the generation that through blindness and indifference destroys the quality of life on our planet.[1]

Charles Lindbergh, 1974

Annual consumption of nonrenewable natural resources if the whole world (4 billion inhabitants) consumed at the same rate as the average American, and length of time it would take for these resources (known recoverable reserves) to be exhausted:

Coal	44 years
Iron	31 years
Nickel	20 years
Bauxite	18 years
Sulphur	12 years
Copper	9 years
Petroleum	7 years
Tin	6 years
Natural gas	5 years
Lead	4 years
Zinc	0.5 years[2]

A Covenant by denominational and ecumenical observers of the United Nations Seventh Special Session, September, 1975:
    We covenant:
    To tithe our time (not for once, those easiest sacrifices of money and compassion) in discipline and self-education, and

family, social and community education, to the end that an
informed body of citizens can jointly take action to see to it
that political and commercial decisions in the U. S. are made in
the light of the Gospel imperative of love and justice;

To bring our lifestyles into balance with God's law of stewardship, seriously examining our individual and corporate
uses of this earth's resources in light of humanity's needs, and
refusing to fulfill our individual and corporate wants at the
price of any person's needs;

*To look at this world with open eyes and to hear its people
with open ears,* no longer "turning off" when what we see and
what we hear is too painful or threatening, but seeing and
listening until we know that we too are among the oppressed,
as well as among the oppressors, so that the Spirit can find
room in us to help us;

To dare to be alive, to risk turning from the false "securities"
we have held on to so long, to dare to ask new questions so
that we may find new answers, to find our deepest joy in the
full humanity of each of our sisters and brothers.

And he sat down opposite the treasury, and watched the
multitude putting money into the treasury. Many rich people
put in large sums. And a poor widow came, and put in two
copper coins, which make a penny. And he called his disciples
to him, and said to them, "Truly, I say to you, this poor widow
has put in more than all those who are contributing to the
treasury. For they all contributed out of their abundance; but
she out of her poverty has put in everything she had, her
whole living."

MARK 12:41-44, RSV

The point is this: he who sows sparingly will also reap sparingly, and he who sows bountifully will also reap bountifully.
Each one must do as he has made up his mind, not reluctantly
or under compulsion, for God loves a cheerful giver. And God
is able to provide you with every blessing in abundance, so

that you may always have enough of everything and may provide in abundance for every good work.

2 CORINTHIANS 9:6-8, RSV

11/8/81

This is how one should regard us, as servants of Christ and
stewards of the mysteries of God.

1 CORINTHIANS 4:1, RSV

Worship Comtee
Silent prayer for Mary Roberto & family

God, we've seen it work. A gift given in love whether it
was money, time, caring, or skill, has been multiplied
by you to meet the needs of others and return an even
larger portion of what I needed to me. Miracles do
happen daily, so I know my attitude and substance of
giving has a lot to do with feeding a world hungry.

I know it has been around a long time, but
stewardship is probably one of the most
misunderstood concepts for Christians today. We drop
our dollar in the plate yet spend ten, twenty, or more
on a dinner out and think nothing of it. Where is our
sense of priorities? You have entrusted to us the
vastness and wonder of this created world.

We are to be responsible for the care of the earth, yet
too often our "dominion" has been to its detriment.
With the advent of our scientific age, we moderns find
it hard to believe that human existence depends on the
earth's fertility—but it does.

The earth provides every substance necessary for life.
In our political maneuvering and striving to control
and protect our boundaries, too often we forget that
the strength of a nation is closely linked to the
soundness of its agriculture.

STEWARDSHIP

As trustee of this planet, as stewards of your
mysteries, as servants of Christ in the world, we do
have concern about exploitation, ignorance, and
indifference, all of which can blight your promise.

Forgive us our apathy. Renew our sense of
servanthood. Strengthen our trustworthiness.

Most of all, restore our faith and hope in your
providence as we seek to live, practice, and learn what
it really means to be a servant people.
                              Amen.

FOR FURTHER PRAYER AND ACTION

1. Seriously try tithing your income for a month. If no
   one in your family suffers, keep it up.
2. Give more of everything than you think you can. Expect good things to come from it.
3. Take the covenant in this chapter yourself. Post it in a
   conspicuous place.
4. Does your place of employment reflect good stewardship of resources? If not, what can you do to help?

135

TECHNOLOGY

The earth can no longer accommodate the sort of society we are building on its surface with the aid of science and technology. It has inbuilt into it self-destructive features. "Our present method of underwriting technology" says Kenneth Galbraith "is exceedingly dangerous. It could cost us our existence." The overriding question now is whether we can obtain control of ourselves and the technology we have created.[1]

CHARLES BIRCH, BIOLOGIST,
Sydney University

Because we now know that the resources of the earth are finite and that the biosphere is not infinitely forgiving, each generation must act as trustee for the next, or at some point there will certainly be no next generation. We are the first generation to have awareness that man has the power to end history, and the first that has the destructive technology to end it ourselves.[2]

RICHARD BARNET AND
RONALD MÜLLER

Recommendations to the churches on "Quality of Life," Fifth Assembly of the World Council of Churches:

1. We call the attention of the churches about the growing concern over the consequences of modern science-based technological developments with its accompaniment of a de-

teriorating environment and debased and alienating forms of human communities. This has resulted in a new call to consider the "quality of life." This is an emphasis on the quality rather than the quantity of material things and on the obligation of the affluent both to provide basic necessities for all the people of planet Earth, and to modify their own consumption patterns, so as to reduce their disproportionated and spiritually destructive drain on earth's non-renewable and renewable resources, excessive use of energy resulting in contamination of the sea and air, and urban concentration and rural poverty that are breeding grounds of starvation, crimes and despair.

2. In solidarity with all who share our concern for quality of life, we encourage churches and Christians to take action to alter those structures and practices which hinder the achievement of an appropriate quality of life.

3. We ask all Christians to take costly and exemplary actions to show by deeds and words their solidarity with and concern for those who are deprived of adequate quality of life.

4. We urge Christians, individually and corporately, to pray for grace and courage to persist in the task of working obediently for the restoration of creation.[3]

And God said, "Let the earth put forth vegetation, plants yielding seed, and fruit trees bearing fruit in which is their seed, each according to its kind, upon the earth." And it was so. The earth brought forth vegetation, plants yielding seed according to their own kinds, and trees bearing fruit in which is their seed, each according to its kind. And God saw that it was good.

GENESIS 1:11-12, RSV

So then, obey the commands that I have given you today; love the Lord your God and serve him with all your heart. If you do, he will send rain on your land when it is needed, in the autumn and in the spring, so that there will be grain, wine,

and olive oil for you, and grass for your cattle. You will have all
the food you want.

DEUTERONOMY 11:13-15, TEV

And Jesus called them to him and said to them, "You know
that those who are supposed to rule over the Gentiles lord it
over them, and their great men exercise authority over them.
But it shall not be so among you; but whoever would be great
among you must be your servant, and whoever would be first
among you must be slave of all. For the Son of man also came
not to be served but to serve, and to give his life as a ransom
for many."

MARK 10:42-45, RSV

**Lord, I read where the view of many scientists and
technologists is that the world is on a catastrophic
course leading to mass starvation, global depletion of
resources, and global environmental deterioration.**

**Guide us in making a deliberate transition to a
sustainable global society in which science and
technology will be mobilized to meet the basic physical
and spiritual needs of people, to minimize suffering
and to create an environment which can sustain a
decent quality of life for all people.**

**Lord, this will surely involve new and more
appropriate technologies, new uses for technology,
and a new sense of social responsibility. I am not a
technologist, but I know I have responsibility for how
technology is used and developed.**

How will my generation accomplish all that it must:
  • **conserve energy as more fuel is needed for food
    production, heating, and other basics;**

- dispose of nuclear waste and guard against the misuse of this awesome power;
- use military technology and justify the use of valuable resources for potentially destructive purposes;
- deal with the social consequences of invasion of privacy and control of mass communication which technology makes possible;
- deal with the ethical dilemmas of biological experimentation and the effects of technology on abortion, contraception, and euthanasia;
- distribute agricultural technology needed to feed a world hungry;
- manage the control of technology and therefore development;
- lead the church in responding to an ambiguous technological future?

Help us maintain a constant encounter of science and faith as we move towards the twenty-first century. There are ethical issues to deal with openly as science involves the human experience. Help us be in dialogue on the interrelatedness of modern scientific insights and the Christian view of your activity in creation.

Lord, these are big questions that have to do with human survival and the meaning of existence. I know that Christians have important contributions to make. May we not lose sight of our task and our place at this crucial time of history.

Amen.

FOR FURTHER PRAYER AND ACTION

1. Avoid overly-packaged products.
2. Try doing without some convenience appliances that use energy.
3. Plan recreation and vacations which are not overly dependent on technology for "fun." Keep quality of life and renewability in mind.
4. Evaluate your position on the use of nuclear energy in light of the perspective of sustainability of the biosphere.

~ 28 ~

THANKSGIVING

Dean Freudenberger, twenty-seven years an agronomist for the Board of Missions of the United Methodist Church and now a visiting professor at the School of Theology at Claremont, California, tells of times of thanksgiving when he was in Sandoa in what was then the Congo in the late 1950s.

Usually the people would stay close to the fires and in their huts at night being especially cautious about animals and snakes in the dark. But sometimes when Friday afternoon came around and the people had eaten well and worked hard, and the moon was out on warm nights, they would come to dance and celebrate. They did not live with individualism which isolates, but rather in community and harmony, working and singing and dancing together.

Then in February of 1960, the people did not sing and dance any more. They began to worry about independence. The army appeared with guns and planes and United Nations' forces. All the dancing stopped.

In talking of defining *development,* Freudenberger observes that you know it is happening with dignity when the people sing and dance with thanksgiving. When there is security from disease and hunger, and the children are sleeping happily, the people come to dance when the moon is out.

A few months ago my three-year-old son Brian suffered

a tragic burn. He pulled boiling water from the stove onto his arm and side. The rush to the hospital was like reading a drama in a real life episode in *Reader's Digest.* He spent weeks in two hospitals, had two surgeries, makes regular visits to the burn clinic, and wears a special elastic suit to help healing.

At the time of the accident, *thanksgiving* was a word I wanted to forget. I was thankful it wasn't worse, but then and now that seems a shallow thanks.

Over the months, however, a deeper thanks has come. Thanksgiving for the depth of strength, patience, love, and understanding found in all children; thanksgiving for the amazing power of the human body to respond to health; thanksgiving on a deeper level for the miracle and gift of life.

As with so many things in life, it is easy to give thanks when intensely moved, but harder on a regular basis. Yet, in the perspective of a world hungry, we have cause for thanksgiving every day. We have cause, too, to pray daily for those who seem to have little reason to give thanks.

> Enter his gates with thanksgiving,
>   and his courts with praise!
>   Give thanks to him, bless his name!

PSALM 100:4, RSV

You will have all you want to eat, and you will give thanks to the Lord your God for the fertile land that he has given you. Make certain that you do not forget the Lord your God; do not fail to obey any of his laws that I am giving you today.

So then, you must never think that you have made yourselves wealthy by your own power and strength. Remember that it is the Lord your God who gives you the power to become rich. He does this because he is still faithful today to the covenant that he made with your ancestors.

DEUTERONOMY 8:10-11, 17-18, TEV

THANKSGIVING

And God, who supplies seed for the sower and bread to eat,
will also supply you with all the seed you need and will make it
grow and produce a rich harvest from your generosity. He will
always make you rich enough to be generous at all times, so
that many will thank God for your gifts which they receive
from us. For this service you perform not only meets the needs
of God's people, but also produces an outpouring of grateful
thanks to God.

2 CORINTHIANS 9:10-12, TEV

Lord, only one in ten returned to give thanks or so the
story goes about the lepers you healed. It is tragic but
I confess, Lord, that 's probably my percentage
compared to the times I ought to be thanking you.

Life has its down turns when I am moved to pray, but
it has more joy and therefore more cause to rejoice
with thanksgiving. In my life I am discovering deeper
thanks, or perhaps understanding more what giving
thanks is all about, as I experience life in more
profound dimensions.

I've been thinking more too about the countless
millions who are more justified than me in keeping
their thanksgiving in. Those whose children cry at
night from pain, those whose parents die too soon.

When the world seems devoid of hope, it is hard to
give thanks. Realistically, I cannot blame them. Yet, I
hear of many who faithfully stay together helping one
another, who, despite living in the streets and eating
the discards of others, sacrifice what they have so
others may survive. For these I give thanks.

VISIONS OF A WORLD HUNGRY

I hear of others who despite persecution and risk of
death stay to minister and serve the poor and hungry
in your name, all the while giving thanks for your love
and bounty. For these I give thanks.

To the one leper who returned and gave thanks you
said, "Your faith has made you well." Your salvation
brought healing which restored him to God. Now clean
he could find meaningful work and return to a full life.

Oh, the miracle of thanksgiving brought to us in the
lessons of life. Praise and majesty be yours, Lord. For
the healing of thanksgiving, thank you.

Amen.

FOR FURTHER PRAYER AND ACTION

1. Let children express their understanding and concern
   about hunger in collages. Display them.
2. Live each day as if it were a precious gift received but
   once. It is.
3. Have an ecumenical community-wide Thanksgiving
   Service in a public place.
4. Practice thanking God consciously many times a day
   for persons and things you are privileged to share.

VALUES

It began early last year. Several national magazines carried an ad by Smith-Corona showing an older teen-age boy beaming Normal Rockwell style, sitting in an over-sized stuffed chair with a new electric typewriter on his lap Christmas morning. He was dressed in a white shirt and tie. The caption below read, "When I was a child, I spake as a child, I understood as a child, I thought as a child: but when I became a man, I put away childish things" (1 Corinthians 13:11).

Now a typewriter company claims its place as that which completes the human experience and brings wholeness and spiritual maturity to fruition.

This is the season of the rape of the scriptures—and all else religious—to appeal to that basic nature of ours (which we try to cover with glibness and gloss) which goes by names such as pride, greed, covetousness, but which only the Bible honestly proclaims as sin. Ironic isn't it? The very condition the Christ Child came to save us from is used as the major ploy to help keep his season alive—at least in the sense of being prosperous.

"Peace on Earth," the store windows proclaim to lull the shoppers into feeling secure in a world and nation full of deep-seated racism, violence, and mistrust. "Goodwill towards men," they shout so you will spend more to somehow make it come true.

Peace and goodwill are as much a longing hope now as when God's messengers heralded it to bewildered shepherds. And that is the tragedy the fourth quarter jump in sales ironically perpetuates. Oh, that we would pay as much attention to developing human dignity and self-worth as we do the latest from Neiman-Marcus. Oh, that the eradication of ignorance, poverty, hunger, and illness would be pursued with half the energy and money that goes into sending cards that herald a shallow greeting and cheap peace. Oh, that publishers would show some integrity, intelligence, and principle, and not push the banalities of Madison Avenue which insult and distort the message of the Prince of Peace.

Whether hunger or any other complex human condition is to be changed depends on *our* values and *our* priorities and whether we think they are ultimately important enough to risk speaking and acting upon.

I know at least one Man who thought they were. Thank God there have been others as well.

> It's one thing to get up
> in the morning and say,
> "This is a new day.
> What am I going to do?"
> But to get up in the morning
> and say,
> "This is my life, my existence.
> What am I doing with it?"
> That's another matter.

Priorities are reflected in the things we spend money on. Far from being a dry accounting of bookkeepers, a nation's budget is full of moral implications; it tells what a society cares about and what it does not care about, it tells what its values are.

J. W. FULBRIGHT, U.S. SENATOR

The kingdom of heaven is like treasure hidden in a field, which a man found and covered up; then in his joy he goes and sells all that he has and buys that field.

MATTHEW 13:44, RSV

Then Peter spoke up. "Look," he said, "we have left everything and followed you. What will we have?"

Jesus said to them, "You can be sure that when the Son of Man sits on his glorious throne in the New Age, then you twelve followers of mine will also sit on thrones, to rule the twelve tribes of Israel. And everyone who has left houses or brothers or sisters or father or mother or children or fields for my sake, will receive a hundred times more and will be given eternal life. But many who now are first will be last, and many who now are last will be first."

MATTHEW 19:27-30, TEV

No one can serve two masters; for either he will hate the one and love the other, or he will be devoted to the one and despise the other. You cannot serve God and mammon.

MATTHEW 6:24, RSV

You are the people of God; he loved you and chose you for his own. So then, you must clothe yourselves with compassion, kindness, humility, gentleness, and patience. Be tolerant with one another and forgive one another whenever any of you has a complaint against someone else. You must forgive one another just as the Lord has forgiven you. And to all these qualities add love, which binds all things together in perfect unity.

COLOSSIANS 3:12-14, TEV

In a recent world opinion poll a majority in the United States regarded religious beliefs as very important. Yet

147

we live in a culture which seems to determine how people live more than their stated beliefs do. Many are still seeking well-defined rewards that have little to do with real needs—accolades, titles, accoutrements of success— rather than doing something of value in particular.

Lord, I know this is a new age. We are creating a new society, one that is not a bigger-than-life version of the present one, but a new one. And because of that it appears many think that values are up for grabs, too. But there is a limit to how much change we can absorb. We need a few stabilizing forces.

Thank you that there are some values which remain to give perspective to the others.

Peace is one. You desire peace at all levels of our existence—inner peace, environmental peace and stability, social peace and justice. With conflicts abounding around the globe in these arenas and more, peace and goodwill are obviously not outdated. May we who hold the value of *your* peace, remain sensitive and responsive enough to take the bold steps necessary to further its reality.

But above all, Lord, there is your love. I pray that the virtues of compassion, kindness, lowliness, meekness, patience, and forgiveness do not get lost in over-sentimentalization or in our rhetoric on love.

When I measure my world with the value of your love, I can almost feel my heart connected to the whole of the cosmos and sense the unity of purpose in which you have allowed me to share.

148

VALUES

Lord, there is doing that needs to be done—solving
the problems of health, poverty, hunger, and more;
based on values which translate into real life decisions
to be made by people who, like me, sometimes find
standing with you pretty tough and lonely in today's
world.

Yes, I know you remember that feeling, too.
Sometimes it is all that keeps me going.

Amen.

FOR FURTHER PRAYER AND ACTION

1. Work toward having your life-style reflect your *true* values.
2. Imagine your house and all its contents burned to the ground. What would remain of value?
3. What values did Christ hold to be most important for life?
4. Are the values we teach children sufficient for the next decade?

VISION

Earth's crammed with heaven,
    And every common bush afire with God;
But only he who sees takes off his shoes;
    The rest sit round it and pluck blackberries.

ELIZABETH BARRETT BROWNING
"Aurora Leigh"

It is the dimensions and clarity of this vision that determine the dimensions of our worlds and the quality of our lives. To the extent that we are blind or have distorted reality, our lives and our happiness have been diminished. Consequently, if we are to change—to grow—there must first be a change in this basic vision, or perception of reality.[1]

JOHN POWELL, S.J., PROFESSOR
Loyola University, Chicago

What matters in the end, it seems to me, is the vision which we each hold in our hearts. That is based, in turn, on what we ultimately believe about our existence in the world. If we believe that the basis of life is a spiritual one, grounded in a loving God, then we will nourish a hope for our future that rests upon his faithfulness as the sacrificial lover of a lost world. We act then, on faith—not with the certain knowledge that our deeds will alter history's course, but with the inner assurance that holding forth such a faith is the first and most important act required of us.[2]

MARK HATFIELD, U.S. SENATOR

VISION

We cannot talk about the lordship of Jesus Christ, or the reconciling love of God, or the meaning of the cross, or Jesus as Liberator, unless the cry of those we treat as non-persons is the central thing we hear, unless the vision of a world so structured as to take them into account is the central thing we see, unless we can come to see the world through their eyes.[3]

ROBERT MCAFEE BROWN,
PROFESSOR
Union Theological Seminary

The eye is the lamp of the body. So, if your eye is sound, your whole body will be full of light; but if your eye is not sound, your whole body will be full of darkness. If then the light in you is darkness, how great is the darkness!

MATTHEW 6:22-23, RSV

I will take delight in Jerusalem and rejoice in my people;
    weeping and cries for help
shall never again be heard in her.
There no child shall ever again die an infant,
    no old man fail to live out his life;
    every boy shall live his hundred years before he dies,
whoever falls short of a hundred shall be despised.
    Men shall build houses and live to inhabit them,
plant vineyards and eat their fruit;

ISAIAH 65:19-21, NEB

Before they call to me, I will answer,
and while they are still speaking I will listen.
The wolf and the lamb shall feed together
and the lion shall eat straw like cattle.
They shall not hurt or destroy in all my holy mountain,
    says the Lord.

ISAIAH 65:24-25, NEB

They said to him, "Lord, let our eyes be opened." And Jesus in pity touched their eyes, and immediately they received their sight and followed him.

MATTHEW 20:33-34, RSV

VISIONS OF A WORLD HUNGRY

My God, thank you for the physical sight to see both light and darkness around me. Thank you too for insight that comes with the vision to tell the difference. I know that my perception of reality, my vision, determines my ability to respond to life, and that the greater my vision, the more fully alive and fully human I can be.

Still I confess that sometimes the smallness of my vision limits my perception of myself, my neighbors, and the world, so that I treat others as less than human and not fully alive—personally, politically, economically, and socially.

Forgive me, O God, for lacking a broader vision. I need a new vision, one that leads to new life: for myself, as I grow and expand my horizons to see even radically different people as part of your love and creation; and for others, whose dreams of enjoying life can be a reality if we share the right vision together.

I need the vision that Jesus gives, that sees no difference between sacred and secular, sexual identity and personhood, ethnic group and worth, economic position and dignity, education and value.

I need the vision to ask the hard questions and to change my attitude and the structures of society where I can. Because of the sensitivity of sight you give, enable me to stand in awe and wonder at life and its possibilities. Help me kneel in humility to worship you and not myself.

Lord, hear me as I say, too, "Let my eyes be opened."
Amen.

VISION

FOR FURTHER PRAYER AND ACTION

1. Resolve to do more than pray about hunger-related issues.
2. Look for personal growth possibilities in new ideas whether you agree with them or not.
3. Look for the presence of God in everything and everybody.
4. Take a quiet walk and appreciate the precious gift of our earth.

❦ 31 ❧

WEALTH

The choice is clear. Either we really become one world, with a problem of policy in certain areas being attacked scientifically on a world scale, or, alternatively, we recognize that there are two worlds—the rich world and the poor—and the latter gets down to the problem of protecting itself against the dominance of the former.

The objectives of the people of the underdeveloped countries can, I think, be summed up in trade union phraseology—fair pay and conditions for a fair day's work.[1]

> PRESIDENT NYERERE OF
> TANZANIA

I want to make it clear in what I propose today that my government fully accepts that the relationship, the balance between the rich and poor countries of the world is wrong and must be remedied . . . that the wealth of the world must be redistributed in favor of the poverty stricken and the starving. This means a new deal in world economics, in trade between nations and the terms of that trade.[2]

> HAROLD WILSON,
> FORMER BRITISH PRIME MINISTER

A society that is declining materially may be ascending spiritually. Perhaps we may be going to return perforce to the way of life of the first Christian monks in Upper Egypt and of their sixth-century Irish successors. The loss of our affluence will be extremely uncomfortable, and it will certainly be difficult to

manage. But in some respects, it may be a blessing in disguise,
if we can rise to the grave occasion.[3]

ARNOLD TOYNBEE

Charles Francis Potter tells about his boys who were children of the parsonage. Some of the wealthier kids sneered at them because they didn't have the finest clothes or toys, so they formed a club of their own made up primarily of the poor kids. They had pup tents and dens in their backyards, and there was a lot of glorious fun.

One day one of the wealthier kids wanted to join the club, and four-year-old Myron asked him to turn around. Then he said, "No, you cannot join. You don't have patches on your pants." And the comment was that the rich boy turned sorrowfully away for he had great possessions but no patches on his pants.

Jesus said to him, "If you would be perfect, go, sell what you possess and give to the poor, and you will have treasure in heaven; and come, follow me." When the young man heard this he went away sorrowful; for he had great possessions.

MATTHEW 19:21-22, RSV

For whoever wants to save his own life will lose it; but whoever loses his life for me and for the gospel will save it. Does a person gain anything if he wins the whole world but loses his life? Of course not! There is nothing he can give to regain his life.

MARK 8:35-37, TEV

Well, religion does make a person very rich, if he is satisfied with what he has. What did we bring into the world? Nothing! What can we take out of the world? Nothing! So then, if we have food and clothes, that should be enough for us. But those

155

who want to get rich fall into temptation and are caught in the trap of many foolish and harmful desires, which pull them down to ruin and destruction. For the love of money is a source of all kinds of evil. Some have been so eager to have it that they have wandered away from the faith and have broken their hearts with many sorrows.

But you, man of God, avoid all these things. Strive for righteousness, godliness, faith, love, endurance, and gentleness.

1 TIMOTHY 6:6-11, TEV

I once heard that the affluent New Yorker may consume twenty-five to fifty thousand times as much energy as a Japanese peasant. *Wealth,* like *poverty,* is a relative term, but there is no doubt that by any global standards I am among the wealthy of the world.

Lord, in my life I have discovered how true Paul's words are to Timothy about the love of money being the root of all evils. I have known so many who have wandered from their faith and who have made themselves and their families suffer immense personal anguish over the pursuit of wealth and its trappings. Yet I know others who can literally buy anything they want who reflect a deep love and concern for their families and others by their humility, generosity, and social conscience.

I have learned that wealth relates to hunger because so much of the world's present economic structure is geared in favor of maintaining the wealthy. I am part of a culture that spends more for personal beautification, jewelry, china, toys and sporting goods, toilet articles, televisions, tobacco, and alcohol *individually* than we do for all developmental aid combined.

WEALTH

Those who first asked and are now demanding a new
economic order involving fairer trade and monetary
agreements are justified as they have looked at the
incongruities and asked, "Why?" I pray for them your
perspective and strength in their struggle. They have
lived with less income, education, life expectancy, and
living children long enough, and are looking to us, the
wealthy, to do something about it.

Lord, I cannot be in church on Sunday and claim I do
not know about them. Maybe I am not wealthy by my
standards, but help me direct my resources to where
they will do the most good. Keep me from judging
those who squander money and parade their wealth.
Enable me to help those afflicted with lust for the
power that wealth brings. Help me remember that it is
far more important to be human than it is to be
important. I love you, Lord.
Amen.

FOR FURTHER PRAYER AND ACTION

1. Make an effort to buy gifts for family and friends from
   Third World countries.
2. If you own stock, find out how your company supports
   a more equitable international economic order. Consider switching from companies that do not think this
   important.
3. In light of what you know about hunger, do you need as
   big a car as you are driving?
4. Does your church budget reflect an awareness of a
   world hungry?

~ 32 ~

WOMEN

Discrimination against women may not directly cause hunger, but it certainly perpetuates it. Of the 700 to 800 million illiterate people in the world, 60 to 70 percent are women. Of the total labor force in the world, 34 percent are women; however, this does not indicate the number of women working. Sixty percent of all the world's farmers are women.

In many of the hungry nations, women have no voice in community or family, political, and economic decisions and receive no education or training in health, nutrition, child care, or farming. Yet they are expected to give birth to, rear, and train all the children and plant, cultivate, and harvest the crops. The woman must also maintain the home and be a good wife. And they must do all this in poverty conditions.

Richard Fagley, a staff member of the World Council of Churches, has said the following:

Over the years, very little attention has been given to helping her find the skills and tools she needs to become a better food producer and preparer, with better conservation of her energy, and better nutrition for her family. The long neglect of her needs and claims is, to my mind, the most outrageous sin of both national and international strategies for development

WOMEN

and for the extension of basic human rights. The time is overdue to overcome this neglect.

Our own United States Commission on Civil Rights has stated that three-fourths of those receiving public assistance and welfare payments are women. That percentage would drop if more jobs were made available, discrimination in hiring were reduced, and child care services were made readily available for mothers who choose to work. The decade of 1975 to 1985 has been designated as the International Women's Decade with these emphases:

- **promote equality between men and women**
- **ensure the full integration of women in the total development effort**
- **recognize the importance of women's increasing contribution to peace**

These goals have a lot to do with feeding a hungry world.

Just then his disciples came. They marveled that he was talking with a woman, but none said, "What do you wish?" or, "Why are you talking with her?"

JOHN 4:27, RSV

Judge not, that you be not judged. For with the judgment you pronounce you will be judged, and the measure you give will be the measure you get.

MATTHEW 7:1-2, RSV

For as many of you as were baptized into Christ have put on Christ. There is neither Jew nor Greek, there is neither slave nor free, there is neither male nor female; for you are all one in Christ Jesus.

GALATIANS 3:27-28, RSV

VISIONS OF A WORLD HUNGRY

Lord, it seems incredible that in our country
discrimination against women and girls occurs in all
areas of American life—economic, legal, political,
educational, in employment, and more. More women are
working yet the gap in wages has actually increased,
even though nearly half of all women are working
because of pressing economic need. Seven and one-half
million widows and single women over sixty-five make
up the poorest segment of American society.

Lord, the church accepts the theory that men and
women were created as equally responsible persons to
glorify you and do your will, but in truth we often ignore
it in practice.

O God, may we faithfully clarify the biblical texts
relating to the role of women in creation and
redemption. May we be more inclusive in imagery and
language to reflect the depth of the mystery which
surrounds you—you who transcend all human
metaphors. May we eliminate sexist patterns in liturgy
and practice so women may join more fully in the
worshiping community.

Internationally, may we support the International
Women's Year and the ten-year plan for action. May we
work to provide funds for self-development and self-help
programs, especially for rural women who are treated
more like favorite cattle than persons of worth and
equality.

As the Body of Christ, help us to affirm positively the
interdependence of men and women and all peoples'
need to feel independent, valuable, and secure in their
identity.

WOMEN

Help us foster respect for persons living in different life situations—single parents and other singles, extended families, and persons in communal arrangements. Let us be inclusive and recognize their special needs. May all denominations give priority to opening the church completely to full ordination and employment opportunities for women.

Lord, I know that sexism, like racism, is a sensitive issue and very hard for many to admit and change attitudes about even though they try hard. May you help us realize how imperative it is to deal lovingly yet forcefully with this issue. May we sense the urgency of our response for the needs of a world hungry and for the unity of the church.

With Paul, I pray that there be neither male nor female as we are all one in Christ.
Amen.

FOR FURTHER PRAYER AND ACTION

1. Make a conscious effort to avoid using sexist language thereby raising your consciousness of the role and status of women.
2. Invite a woman clergy to speak to a group in your church.
3. Pray for oppressed women in the world, remembering that more than half the world is decades behind the progress made for women's rights in this country.
4. Encourage children to consider any vocation as being open to them.

STUDY GUIDE FOR
INDIVIDUAL & GROUP USE

Purpose: To help you focus on the biblical and the theological roots of the hunger/justice issue.

Unlike some contemporary issues, we do not have to stretch to make the Bible pertinent to the hunger/justice issue. We find that there are several major themes throughout the Old and New Testaments that give us a strong foundation for understanding it.

As this book implies, hunger is caused and perpetuated by a broad spectrum of factors. While one does not need to master knowledge of them all, a working awareness is essential to focus and appreciate the necessity to respond on several fronts at once. Everyone has some contribution to make that can be significant in conquering hunger and insuring justice and love.

Our purpose in study is not just to find prooftexts or relevant passages that support our concern for the hungry. It is more fundamental than that. It is to discover again, in the total context of our twentieth-century world, the meaning of the gospel for our personal and corporate lives as we deal with this issue.

The study sessions will give you a more coherent perspective on the hunger/justice issue in three essential areas: (1) biblical and theological perspectives; (2) hunger facts; and (3) Christian life-style response. These are all part of the same package—Christian living in today's world. They all grow out of the same event—the love of God as revealed in Jesus Christ.

Two major approaches are generally used in biblical studies. One starts with a life situation then finds the biblical emphases that apply to it. The other begins with the biblical text and finds where it applies to life situation. This study will direct you primarily in the latter for good reason:

1. There are already ample materials on the problem of hunger, its causes and ramifications. There is little on the biblical and moral roots of a Christian's response to it.

2. The hunger/justice issue is so complex that without a strong foundation in the "why" of our response as Christians, we can easily get lost in the issues and lose sight of our direction.

3. Personal response to hunger can be personally taxing as we get more involved, and fighting injustice because of our Christian and moral response can test our faith. We can easily feel overwhelmed or defeated. We can become bitter or depressed after we work so hard but see slower results than we expected. We can feel like quitting because we think we've done our part and that's enough. Yet in the midst of that, our faith can still grow. We can grow in and be strengthened by our knowledge and love of God if we know we are doing God's work and not just our own. Our Christian walk always leads us back to the Bible where we find "strength and help in time of need" and a reason to press on.

4. No matter how well we know the Bible, there is al-

163

ways more to discover. With a perspective of major biblical themes, we can more clearly see God's concern and therefore our own, for every issue and current event of our day. We learn to develop a theological view of the world and our part in it.

As a personal goal, ask yourself, "How do I want to be different as a result of this study?"

To Leaders and Participants

In every successful discussion study group, all participants share responsibility for the group's progress; consequently it is not up to one "leader" to be the teacher. This is especially true in a study of this kind. Each person not only has valuable insights and observations to contribute, but only by each individual participating in the reading of the chapters and the searching of the scripture will they grow.

You will still need a facilitator to get the group going, but don't let them do all the study—otherwise you have defeated your purpose for being in the group.

Some General Suggestions

Meet in a comfortable setting in a circle so everyone can see and hear one another. Provide writing material for each person. Pay attention to each person's contribution as it is being given. Don't spend your time just thinking about what you are going to say—you may miss something valuable. Write key ideas and insights on the blackboard or newsprint for all to clearly see. This will also give you a record of the group's thoughts. Encourage openness and free discussion. Creating and analyzing are two different processes. In this group, all ideas are acceptable as creative. You can analyze and evaluate them later after the group is over.

STUDY GUIDE FOR INDIVIDUAL AND GROUP USE

How to Use the Session Guides

You will not find ready-made answers in this study guide. *You* must search the scriptures to discover where and how the Bible talks about these issues, and you are left to make the connections and applications to these topics and your own life situation in relation to them. The guide is just that—a guide to assist you in doing your own study.

There are four session guides. There is more material in each one than can be covered in one hour, therefore, there is no limit on how much time you spend on each. (You may wish to supplement and/or expand the scope of the sessions by including a more detailed study of hunger facts using one of the suggested resource books in the bibliography.)

Each of the four sessions is divided into four sections as follows:

Theme. This is a one-sentence summary statement of the main theological point. Keep referring back to it in the session to keep from losing direction with side issues.

Background Chapters. These chapters in the book contain material that applies generally to the session theme. They are not rigid, however, because in one way or another all the chapters apply. Therefore, feel free to include other chapters if you think they are pertinent.

Reading the background chapters will give you facts and insights to relate to your discussion.

Perhaps to start the session, members could share a prayer or portions of one they especially identified with in the book.

Biblical Perspective. These statements are derived directly from the scriptures used in the session. They are summary statements of what the Bible is saying. As you study the scripture yourself, use them in two ways:

165

1. You may discover further biblical perspectives that apply. Add them to the list. Or, personalize the perspective by rewriting it in language that makes the point the way you would say it.

2. Ask these questions:
   a. How does each specific biblical passage support one or more of the perspectives?
   b. What do I/my society do to thwart the biblical perspectives?
   c. What do or can I/my society do to fulfill them?

Study Outline. This is a bare-bones outline, the heart of it being the scripture references. Have the group look up all the scripture by dividing them according to number or by letting individuals select a topic in the outline that interests them.

Your purpose is to discover (1) what the individual passage says by itself, (2) how it relates to the other scriptures as a whole, (3) what we can accurately say the Bible is telling us about how we relate to God (biblical perspective), and (4) what that means for our life choices.

Use commentaries to help interpret the passages. Or read the selections from different translations to enrich your understanding of it.

Most importantly, begin where you are, with what you identify with most easily. Other people may make different applications or express other concerns, but with the power and contemporaneity of the scriptures in the context of today, you can begin to see the interrelatedness of your concern to theirs, thereby enabling both of you to broaden and enlighten your knowledge and concern.

At the End of Each Session. Pray together. Pray for each of the group members personally. Pray that God will enrich your study. Pray for a world hungry.

Assign group members book chapters and/or scripture to read in preparation for the next session.

At the End of the Study. Decide as a group what your next course of action will be, either further study of hunger related material, a beginning project to help fight hunger, or a way to involve more people in study groups. Be creative, but *do* something!

Session One
GOD'S PRESENCE IN THE CREATED ORDER

Theme: God is present in the whole of natural and human creation as Creator, Sustainer, and Redeemer, and we share responsibility for that created order's well-being.

Background Chapters: 5,7,8,15,24,27

Biblical Perspectives:

1. Through salvation in Christ, we are made at one with God (at-one-ment). We receive and are called to actualize the potential for wholeness already inherent in the created order.

2. God intends a just order in human existence consistent with the natural created order. We are required to interact with our environment in accordance with God's intentions. It is our responsibility to care for God's creation.

3. God is love. The purpose of our nurturing the human and nonhuman creation is to ensure a harmony that helps people grow in their ability to love as God intended.

Study Outline

I. God as Creator and Sustainer	Deut. 11:11-12
A. God intends a just human order	Pss. 145:8-9; 146:6-7*b*
B. Creation is a gift	Gen. 1:31*a*; 9:2-3 Pss. 24:1; 104:10-15,27-30

C. God supplies in abundance	Gen. 1:11-12
D. We are given authority	Ps. 8
II. God as Redeemer	Deut. 24:14-22
A. Providence	Num. 11:7-9
	Deut. 8:3-5
	2 Kings 4:42-44
	Matt. 15:32-39
B. Deliverance	Num. 11:10-17
C. Obedience	Deut. 11:13-17
D. Covenant	Deut. 11:18-21
E. Thanksgiving	Deut. 26:1-3,10-11
F. Faith	Exod. 16:2-4,12

Session Two
HUMAN EXISTENCE SEEKS LIFE

Theme: The purpose of human existence is life, and God promises a blessing of wholeness on those who seek life and the welfare of the whole human community to which they are related.

Background Chapters: 10,11,14,17,18,20,21,22,32

Biblical Perspectives:

1. God loves and intends justice for all his children. As Christians, therefore, we are global citizens linked to all of humanity.

2. God intends a moral order to pervade human affairs, yet we have disrupted God's creation.

3. We depend on God to give through a complex social system.

4. God loves and cares for the poor and seeks to deliver them. Jesus identified with the poor. With God's help, we are called to be active on their behalf.

168

Study Outline

Within God's order, the purpose of human existence is life.	Isa. 55:1-3 John 6:26-59, 8:12, 10:10*b*, 11:25-26
I. The Basis of Life in Christ	Rom. 5:12-21
A. Love	Lev. 19:18 Ps. 145:13*b*-20 Mark 12:28*b*-31 John 3:16-17, 13:31-35 15:10 1 John 3:16-18, 23-24
B. Wholeness of human existence already present as promise of God's blessing on those who seek life	Mic. 6:8 Matt. 5:3-12, 6:7-15, 7:12, 26-27
C. Concern for the whole human community	Luke 10:29-37, 14:15-24 John 4:27
D. Seeking its welfare	Isa. 2:4 Mark 9:35, 10:42-45
II. God Loves and Cares for the Poor	Isa. 58:1-10, 25:4 Ps. 82:3-5
A. Rights given to all God's children	Deut. 10:12-14, 18-20 Amos 5:21-24
B. God will be active on behalf of the poor	Pss. 146:7-9, 132:15
C. Rights of the poor (justice)	
1. Command to care for poor	Amos 5:11

169

2.	Protect poor	Lev. 19:9-10
		Deut. 15:7-11
3.	No permanent	Lev. 25:11
	debt	Deut. 15:1-2
4.	Freedom in	Lev. 25:39-55
	seventh year	
5.	Not	Deut. 15:12-15
	empty-handed	
6.	Not exploited	Amos. 8:4-7
7.	Equal justice	Exod. 23:4-9
		Deut. 27:19-26
8.	Pluck grain	Exod. 23:10-11
		Deut. 23:25
9.	Tithing	Deut. 14:28-29
D.	Jesus identified	Luke 4:18-19 (Is. 61:1-3)
	with the poor	Luke 4:1-13, 7:22
1.	Association with	Matt. 11:19
	poor	
2.	Adoption of poor	Mark 10:42-45
	life-style	
3.	Sending	Mark 6:8-9
	disciples in	Luke 9:3, 10:4
	poverty	
4.	Acceptance of	Matt. 25:31-46
	self equated with	
	ministry to poor	
5.	Response to	Matt. 6:25-34, 16:5-12
	hungry	
6.	Accumulating	Matt. 6:24
	goods opposed to	Luke 12:16-21
	service to God	

Session Three
HUMAN FREEDOM AND RESPONSIBILITY

Theme: Out of love God created us with human freedom and responsibility and a large choice in determining our own destiny.

Background Chapters: 1,2,6,9,16,23,25,28,29

Biblical Perspectives:

1. The limits of our choices are determined by the order of God's creation, yet we are called to respond to the limits of our God-given capabilities.

2. In Christ we are the beginning of a new creation. Christ exemplified the responsible life that God intends for *every* person.

3. Christ promises an abundant life. We affirm God's way of giving through a right ordering of our individual and corporate lives.

Study Outline

Human Freedom and Responsibility	Matt. 7:16
	Gen. 3:5
I. Role in Determining Own Destiny	2 Cor. 3:2-3
A. Human response to limits of capacity	Matt. 25:14-30
	Mark 4:21-25, 10:31
	Luke 3:10-14, 9:62
	John 13:13-14
	James 1:22
B. Humans share responsibility for created order's well-being	Mark 8:35-37
	John 21:15-16
	James 2:14-17,26
C. Dangers of wealth gathered at others'	Deut. 8:7-20
	Matt. 6:24

171

expense	Luke 12:16-21
	1 Tim. 6:6-11,17-19
1. Leads to	Amos 6:4-6
indifference	Luke 7:47
	John 9:39-41
2. Complicity in	Matt. 23:1-12
oppression	
3. Injustice	Lam. 2:19-20*b*, 4:9-10
	Hab. 2:6-8
	Mark 15:6-14
II. Life-style	Prov. 25:16
	Isa. 3:13-15
	Matt. 5:43-44, 6:1-6
	Mark 1:6, 2:18-22, 12:17
	Rom. 12:20
A. Jesus' demands	Matt. 5:14-16
1. Renounce	Matt. 6:24-33
anxicty of guods	
and trust God	
2. Treasurers	Matt. 6:19-21
3. Willing to leave	Matt. 10:34-36
it all	Luke 14:33
4. Not judging	Matt. 7:1-2
5. Prayer	Matt. 7:9-11
6. Discipleship	Matt. 19:21-22
7. Seek Kingdom	Matt. 6:33
first	
B. Knowledge	Luke 2:41-52
C. Politics	Matt. 5:33-37, 38-42,
	21:33-46
	John 2:13-16
D. Right ordering of	Prov. 14:21, 21:13
individual and	
corporate life	

    E. Helping the poor   Acts 11:27-30
                                   Rom. 15:26-27
                                   1 Cor. 16:1-2

Session Four
FULLNESS OF LIFE A PRESENT GOAL

Theme: Fullness of life for the whole human community is not just a dreamed-of future end point in history, but an active, present goal.
Background Chapters: 3,4,12,13,19,26,30
Biblical Perspectives:
1. God desires quality of life for all persons. The church is the new creation. We are called to participate in God's mission in the world now and to share as a community in ways that address the needs of all of God's children and that enable us to better serve them.
2. Living a full human life in the presence of God is both a future promise and a present reality. To fulfill God's purpose, we are to know and use the resources available to us, appropriate life-styles, and reshape corporate life to justly distribute and care for the earth's resources.

Study Outline
To achieve fullness of life God gives us the following:
    I. Hope   Phil. 4:10-20
   II. Vision   Isa. 40:4, 65:19-25
                         Luke 1:53, 16:19-31
                         1 Tim. 2:4
                         Rev. 21:1-4
 III. The Mission of the   Matt. 9:35-38, 11:1,
       Church   28:20
                         Luke 4:43
                         John 11:51-52
                         1 Cor. 16:4
                         2 Cor. 8:9

IV. Christian Community	John 17:21
	1 Cor. 10:17
	1 John 1:3, 4:20-21
A. To better serve the poor	Mark 9:40-41
B. To share resources	Acts 2:42-47, 4:32
	2 Cor. 8:13-15, 9:6-8
	James 2:1-7
C. To adopt appropriate life-styles	Gal. 2:10
V. The Incarnation	Matt. 26:26-29
	Luke 24:30-35
	John 1:14, 2:23-25, 14:12, 21:12-14
	1 Cor. 11:23-34
	Phil. 2:7-8

NOTES

CHAPTER 1

1. Alvin Toffler, *The Eco-Spasm Report: Why Our Economy Is Running Out of Control* (New York: Bantam Books, 1975), p. 106.

2. Arthur Simon, *Bread for the World* (Grand Rapids: Wm. B. Eerdmans, 1975), p. 137.

CHAPTER 2

1. Erik Eckholm and Frank Record, *Worldwatch Paper No. 9* (Washington: Worldwatch Institute, 1976).

CHAPTER 3

1. Preliminary reports, Section I, Chapter 3, Fifth Assembly of the World Council of Churches, Nairobi, Kenya, 1975.

2. Mortimer Arias, "That the World May Believe," 27 November 1975, address to World Council of Churches.

CHAPTER 4

1. Parker J. Palmer, "A Place Called Community," *Christian Century*, 16 March 1977, p. 253.

2. Shridath S. Ramphal, "On A Larger Scale," *Ceres*, FAO, Jan.–Feb. 1976, p. 45.

3. Mark Hatfield, *Between a Rock and a Hard Place* (Waco, Texas: Word, 1976), p. 184. Used by permission of Word Books, Publisher, Waco, Texas 76703.

4. Elizabeth O'Connor, *The New Community* (New York: Harper & Row), 1976, p. 1.

CHAPTER 5

1. Barbara Ward and Rene Dubos, *Only One Earth: The Care and Maintenance of a Small Planet* (New York: Norton, 1972), p. 12.

175

2. Charles Birch, "Creation, Technology and Human Survival: Called to Replenish the Earth," 1 December 1975, address to Fifth Assembly WCC.

CHAPTER 8

1. Frances M. Lappé, *Diet for a Small Planet* (New York: Friends of the Earth/Ballantine Books, 1971), p. 3.

2. *An Alternate Diet*, pamphlet published by Bread for the World. *Time magazine*, 11 November 1974.

CHAPTER 9

1. "Human Rights and Christian Responsibility," Human Rights Background Document, Commission of the Churches on International Affairs of the WCC, p. 80.

2. Charles Birch, "Creation, Technology and Human Survival: Called to Replenish the Earth."

3. Robert McAfee Brown, "Who Is This Jesus Christ Who Frees and Unites?" 25 November 1975, address to Fifth Assembly WCC.

CHAPTER 10

1. Mark Hatfield, *Between a Rock and a Hard Place*, p. 193. Used by permission of Word Books, Publisher, Waco, Texas 76703.

CHAPTER 12

1. C. Dean Freudenberger, "Our Global Hunger Concern," 5 October 1975 speech in Oklahoma City.

2. Maurice Strong, Statement to Fifth Assembly WCC, 8 December 1975.

CHAPTER 13

1. Sartaz Azia, "The World Food Situation Now and in the Year 2000," 28 June 1976 address to World Food Conference, Ames, Iowa.

2. Edouard Saouma, *Ceres*, Jan.–Feb. 1976, p. 27.

3. Encyclical Letter of His Holiness Pope Paul VI On the Development of Peoples, 1967.

CHAPTER 14

1. Report of Section VI, "Human Development: Ambiguity of Power, Technology and Quality of Life," Introduction, Fifth Assembly WCC, 1975.

2. Martin Luther King, Jr., in *The Trumpet of Conscience*, 1967, p. 77 (from *Patriot's Bible*, p. 116).

3. Arthur Simon, *Bread for the World*, p. 75.

CHAPTER 16

1. Norman Borlaug, at Bread for the World Board Meeting, May 1977, quoted in Bread for the World newsletter, June 1977.

2. Charles Birch, "Creation, Technology and Human Survival."

CHAPTER 17

1. Helmut Thielicke, *African Diary* (Waco, Texas: Word, 1974), p. 32.

CHAPTER 18

1. Dwight D. Eisenhower, in his "Cross of Iron" April 1953, speech (from *Patriot's Bible*, p. 141).

2. A Study Action Packet for World Development, New International Publications. ("All material in this publication may be freely reproduced with appropriate acknowledgment" to Stage House, High Street, Benson, Oxon, OX9 6 RP, United Kingdom).

CHAPTER 20

1. Lester Brown, *Worldwatch Paper No. 8* (Washington: Worldwatch Institute, 1976), p. 31.

CHAPTER 21

1. Ernest F. Hollings, in Bread for the World filmstrip.

2. Peter Adamson, "Consensus on Crisis," *New Internationalist*, October 1975, pp. 1-2.

3. Poverty Profile quoted in *Patriot's Bible*, p. 9.

CHAPTER 22

1. Arthur Simon, *Bread for the World*, p. 86.

CHAPTER 23

1. Bruce Birch, *Christian Century*, 11-18 June 1975.

CHAPTER 25

1. Philip Potter, General Secretary's Report, 1975, Fifth Assembly WCC.

CHAPTER 26⁻

1. Charles Lindbergh in May 1977 article "Lindbergh Alone," by Brendan Gill. *Reader's Digest.*
2. Chart, from *Ceres,* March–April 1976, p. 20.

CHAPTER 27

1. Charles Birch, "Creation, Technology and Human Survival."
2. Richard Barnet and Ronald Muller, in "Global Reach," (*New Yorker,* December 9, 1974) pp. 156-157 (from *Patriot's Bible,* p. 175).
3. Section VI, Sub-section D: Recommendations, "Quality of Life," Fifth Assembly, WCC, 1975.

CHAPTER 30

1. John Powell, S.J., *Fully Human, Fully Alive* (Niles, Illinois: Argus Communications, 1976), p. 10.
2. Mark Hatfield, *Between a Rock and a Hard Place,* p. 167. Used by permission of Word Books, Publisher, Waco, Texas 76703.
3. Robert McAfee Brown, "Who Is This Jesus Who Frees and Unites?"

CHAPTER 31

1. Nyerere, quoted in *New Internationalist,* October 1975, p. 16.
2. Wilson, quoted in *New Internationalist,* October 1975, p. 15.
3. Arnold Toynbee, article in *Faith at Work,* August 1975, p. 21. This quote originally appeared in *The Observer,* of London, England.

RESOURCES
FOR STUDY & ACTION

This resource list is a beginning place to find further information and groups that concern hunger. Many more resources could be listed. For suggestions on where to start for yourself, see the Study Guide.

1. BASIC BOOKS

*Brown, Lester, *By Bread Alone*, Praeger Publishers, New York, 1974. With Erik Eckholm, these two leading authorities on hunger define the dimensions of the problem, discuss the basic resources to meet it, offer some areas of hope and give specific recommendations for response. 253 pp.

*Freudenberger, C. Dean and Minus, Paul, *Christian Responsibility in a Hungry World*, Abingdon Press, Nashville, 1976. An expert agronomist and theologian state succinctly the root causes of hunger and offer a theological framework on which to respond as well as pragmatic suggestions. 128 pp.

*Sider, Ronald J., *Rich Christians in an Age of Hunger*. Inter-Varsity Press, Downers Grove, Illinois, 1977. A conservative biblical scholar gives a very broadminded and helpful analysis of the hunger problem and a thorough yet easy-to-read picture of the biblical mandate for response. 174 pp.

*Simon, Arthur, *Bread for the World*, Wm. B. Eerdmans Publishing Co., Grand Rapids, 1975. The Director of Bread for the World offers penetrating insights into the dimensions of hunger with helpful response ideas. 177 pp.

2. OTHER HUNGER-RELATED REFERENCES

Barbour, Ian G., ed., *Finite Resources and the Human Future*, Augsburg Publishing House, Minneapolis, Minn. 1976.

Barnet, Richard J., and Muller, Ronald E., *Global Reach, The Power of the Multinational Corporations.*, Simon & Shuster, New York, 1975.

Berg, Alan, *The Nutrition Factor*, Brookings, Washington, D.C., 1973.

Biéler, André, *The Politics of Hope*, Wm. B. Eerdmans Publishing Co., Grand Rapids, 1974.

Brown, Lester R., *In the Human Interest*, Norton, New York, 1974.

——————, *The Twenty-Ninth Day*, Norton, New York, 1978.

——————, *World Without Borders*, Random House, New York, 1973.

Brown, Lester R., and Finsterbusch, Gail, *Man and His Environment: Food*, Harper & Row, New York, 1972.

Câmara, Dom Hélder, *Revolution Through Peace*, Harper Colophon Books, New York, 1972.

Clark, Dennis E., *The Third World and Mission*, Word Books, Waco, Texas, 1971.

Clark, Wilson, *Energy for Survival.* Doubleday, New York, 1975.

Commoner, Barry, *The Closing Circle*, Bantam Books, New York, 1972.

Connelly, Philip, and Perlman, Robert, *The Politics of Scarcity*, Oxford University Press, London, 1975.

Costas, Orlando E., *The Church and Its Mission: A Shattering Critique from the Third World*, Tyndale, Wheaton, Illinois, 1975.

Eckholm, Erik P., *The Picture of Health: Environmental Sources of Disease*, Norton, New York, 1977.

——————, *Losing Ground: Environmental Stress and World Food Prospects*, Norton, New York, 1978.

Elliot, Charles, *Patterns of Poverty in the Third World*, Praeger Publishers, New York, 1975.

——————, *The Development Debate*, Friendship Press, New York, 1971.

Gheddo, Pierro, *Why Is the Third World Poor?* tr. Kathryn Sullivan, Orbis Books, Maryknoll, New York, 1973.

Hatfield, Mark, *Between a Rock and a Hard Place*, Word Books, Waco, Texas, 1976.

Hayes, Dennis, *Rays of Hope, The Transition to a Post-Petroleum World*, Norton, New York, 1977.

RESOURCES FOR STUDY AND ACTION

Heilbroner, Robert L., *An Inquiry into the Human Prospect*, Norton, New York, 1974.

Lappé, Frances Moore, and Collins, Joseph, *Food First: Beyond the Myth of Scarcity*, Houghton Mifflin, Boston, 1977.

Laszlo, Ervin, et. al., *Goals for Mankind, A Report to the Club of Rome on the New Horizons of Global Community*, E. P. Dutton, New York, 1977.

*Lerza, Catherine, and Jacobson, Michael, eds., *Food for People Not for Profit*, Ballentine Books, New York, 1975.

Lucas, George R., and Ogletree, Thomas, eds., *Lifeboat Ethics: The Moral Dilemma of World Hunger*, Harper Forum Books, New York, 1976.

McNamara, Robert S., *One Hundred Countries, Two Billion People: The Dimensions of Development*, Praeger Publishing, New York, 1973.

Meadows, Donella H., et al., *The Limits to Growth; A Report for the Club of Rome on the Predicament of Mankind*, Universe Books, New York, 1974.

Mesarovic, Mihajlo, and Pestel, Eduard, *Mankind at the Turing Point: The Second Report to the Club of Rome*, E. P. Dutton & Co. Inc., New York, 1974.

*Mooneyham, Stanley, *What Do You Say to a Hungry World?*, Word Books, Waco, Texas, 1975.

Myrdal, Gunnar, *The Challenge of World Poverty*, Vintage Books, New York, 1971.

Paton, David M., ed., *Breaking Barriers, Nairobi 1975*, Wm. B. Eerdmans Publishing, Grand Rapids, 1976. World Council of Churches.

Rich, William, *Smaller Families Through Social and Economic Progress*, Overseas Development Council, 1973, Monograph No. 7.

Sartarius, Peter, *Churches in Rural Development, Guidelines for Action*, World Council of Churches, 1975.

*Seifert, Harvey, *Good News for Rich and Poor*, United Church Press, Philadelphia, 1976.

Simon, Paul, and Simon, Arthur, *The Politics of World Hunger*, Harper & Row, New York, 1973.

Thielicke, Helmut, *African Diary*, Word Books, Waco, Texas, 1974.

Tofler, Alvin, *The Eco-Spasm Report*, Bantam Books, New York, 1975.

VISIONS OF A WORLD HUNGRY

Ward, Barbara, and Dubos, Rene, *Only One Earth*, W. W. Norton & Co., Inc., New York, 1972.

Ward, Barbara, *Rich Nations and the Poor Nations*, W. W. Norton & Co. Inc., New York, 1962.

_____, *My Lopsided World*, W. W. Norton & Co. Inc., 1968.

What Do We Do for Lifeboats When the Ship Goes Down?, Harper Colophon Books, New York, 1976.

Worldwatch Papers, Worldwatch Institute, 1776 Massachusetts Avenue, N.W., Washington, D.C. 20036

No.   1. *The Other Energy Crisis: Firewood*, Erik Eckholm

No.   2. *The Politics and Responsibility of the North American Breadbasket*, Lester Brown

No.   3. *Women in Politics: A Global Review*, Kathleen Newland

No.   4. *Energy: The Case for Conservation*, Denis Hayes

No.   5. *Twenty-Two Dimensions of the Population Problem*, Lester Brown, Patricia McGrath, Bruce Stokes

No.   6. *Nuclear Power: The Fifth Horseman*, Denis Hayes

No.   7. *The Unfinished Assignment: Equal Education for Women*, Patricia McGrath

No.   8. *World Population Trends· Signs of Hope, Signs of Stress*, Lester Brown

No.   9. *The Two Faces of Malnutrition*, Erik Eckholm Frank Record

No.   10. *Health: The Family Planning Factor*, Erik Eckholm, Kathleen Newland

No.   11. *Energy: The Solar Prospect*, Denis Hayes

No.   12. *Filling the Family Planning Gap*, Bruce Stokes

No.   13. *Spreading Deserts, The Hand of Man*, Erik Eckholm, Lester Brown

No.   14. *Redefining National Security*, Lester Brown

No.   15. *Energy for Development: Third World Options*, Dennis Hayes

No.   16. *Women and Population Growth: Choice Beyond Childbearing*, Kathleen Newland

No.   17. *Local Responses to Global Problems: A Key to Meeting Basic Human Needs*, Bruce Stokes

No.   18. *Cutting Tobacco's Toll*, Erik Eckholm

No.   19. *The Solar Energy Timetable*, Dennis Hayes

No.   20. *The Global Economic Prospect: New Sources of Economic Stress*, Lester Brown

3. BIBLICAL AND THEOLOGICAL REFERENCES

Anderson, Gerald, and Stansky, Thomas, eds., *Mission Trends*, New York and Wm. B. Eerdmans, Grand Rapids.
No. 1. Critical Issues in Mission Today
No. 2. Evangelization
No. 3. Third World Theologies
Batey, Richard, *Jesus and the Poor*, Harper & Row, New York, 1972.
Bonhoeffer, Dietrich, *The Cost of Discipleship*, Macmillan Co., New York, 1963.
Chamberlain, David, *How Jesus Loved*, 1971.
Cobb, John B., *God and the World*, Westminster Press, Philadelphia, 1969.
Cogswell, James A., ed., *The Church and the Rural Poor*, John Knox Press, Atlanta, 1975.
Conzelmann, Hans, *Jesus*, tr. J. Raymond Lord, Fortress Press, Philadelphia, 1973.
Derr, Thomas, *Ecology and Human Need*, Westminster Press, Philadelphia, 1975.
Dickinson, Richard D.N., *To Set at Liberty the Oppressed*, Commission on the Churches Participation in Development, WCC, 1975.
Freire, Paulo, *Pedagogy of the Oppressed*, tr. Myra B. Ramos, Seabury Press, New York, 1971.
Goulet, Denis, *A New Moral Order*, Orbis Books, New York, 1974.
Gutierrez, Gustavo, *A Theology of Liberation*, tr. Caridad Cluda, Sr. and John Eagleson, Orbis Books, Maryknoll, New York, 1973.
Hellwig, Monika, *The Eucharist and the Hunger of the World*, Paulist Press, New York, 1976.
Hengel, Martin, *Property and Riches in the Early Church*, tr. John Bowden, Fortress Press, Philadelphia, 1975.
Koyama, Kosuke, *Waterbuffalo Theology*, Orbis Books, Maryknoll, New York, 1974.
Minear, Larry, *New Hope for the Hungry?*, Friendship Press, New York, 1975.
Moltmann, Jurgen, *The Gospel of Liberation*, tr. H. Wayne Pipkin, Word Books, Waco, Texas, 1973.
O'Conner, Elizabeth, *Journey Inward, Journey Outward*, Harper & Row, New York, 1975.
_____, *The New Community*, Harper & Row, New York, 1976.

Owens, Owen D., *Stones Into Bread?*, Judson Press, Valley George, Pennsylvania, 1977.

Segundo, Juan Luis, *The Liberation of Theology*, Orbis Books, Maryknoll, New York, 1976.

Taylor, John V., *Enough Is Enough*, Augsburg Publishing House, Minneapolis, 1977.

Taylor, Richard K., *Economics and the Gospel*, United Church Press, Philadelphia, 1973.

Yoder, John Howard, *The Politics of Jesus*, Wm. B. Eerdmans, Grand Rapids, 1972.

4. RESOURCES FOR RESPONSE
(In addition other books marked with * have sections on response.)

Crouch, Timothy J., and Dessun, Ralph E., *Hunger Workbook*, C.S.S. Publishing Co., Lima, Ohio, 1977. More than one hundred ideas presenting the problems of world hunger.

Ewald, Ellen Buchman, *Recipes for a Small Planet*, Ballentine Books, New York, 1973. Expands philosophy of *Diet for a Small Planet* with hundreds of specific recipes.

From the Ground Up: Building a Grass Roots Food Policy, Center for Science in the Public Intercst, 1976. A handbook for action for those wishing to reform the food policies of their city, county or state.

Kaysing, Bill and Ruth, *Eat Well on a Dollar a Day*, Chronicle Books, San Francisco, 1975. Basic facts and hints on nutrition, gardening, budgeting, and buying and simplified eating.

Lapp e, Frances Moore, *Diet for a Small Planet*, Ballentine Books, New York, 1975. The cause of hunger; our responses and suggestions for protein rich recipes.

Longacre, Doris Janzen, *More-With-Less Cookbook*, Herald Press, Scottdale, Pennsylvania, 1976. Suggestions by Mennonites on how to eat better and consume less of the world's limited food resources.

99 Ways to a Simple Lifestyle, Center for Science in the Public Interest, 1976. Practical suggestions for heating and cooling, energy conservation, food, gardening, clothing, health, transportation, and more.

Runk, Wesley T., *Who Needs a Bigger Barn?*, C.S.S. Publishing Co., Lima, Ohio, 1977. Five story sermons on hunger for children.

Seifert, Harvey and Lois, *Liberation of Life, Growing Exercises in*

RESOURCES FOR STUDY AND ACTION

Meditation and Action, Upper Room, Nashville, 1976. A guide to
meditation and action for individuals and groups on Christian
life-styles.

Especially for Teachers and Parents

Educating for Peace and Justice, A Resource for Teachers, Institute
for Education in Peace and Justice, 3700 West Pine, St. Louis,
Mo. 63108. A curriculum for teaching about peace, justice,
economics, hunger, military for public and religious schools.

Goodwin, Mary T., and Pollen, Gerry, *Creative Food Experiences
for Children,* Center for Science in the Public Interest, 1974.
Activity and information book for leaders and teachers of children
from pre-school on up. Teaches basics of good nutrition and consumption with fun activities.

Katz, et. al., *Food: Where Nutrition, Politics and Culture Meet,*
CSPI, 1976. An activity book for teachers of children of all ages on
eating patterns, nutrition, food consumption and supply, global
and domestic hunger.

Millar, Jayne C., *Focusing on Global Poverty and Development,*
Overseas Development Council, 1974. A complete resource book
for teachers of older elementary, secondary and college students
on all aspects of the hunger/justice issue.

World Hunger, A Unit for Teachers, 1976. Institute for Education
in Peace and Justice, 1976. A short, but effective, list of classroom
activites for action pertinent to younger students.

5. PERIODICALS AND NEWSLETTERS

Ceres, U.N. Food and Agricultural Organization's monthly review
on Agricultural and Development. Order from UNIPUB, 650
First Avenue, P.O. Box 433, Murray Hill Station, New York, NY
10016.

Environmental Action Bulletin, 33 E. Minor St. Emmaus, Pa.
18049. Bi-weekly newsletter written by Robert Rodale on environmental issues and legislation.

Food Monitor, published by World Hunger Year and Institute for
Food and Development Policy, P.O. Box 1975, Garden City, New
York 11530.

Impact, Newsletter published by Interreligion Taskforce on U.S.
Food Policy, 110 Maryland Avenue, N.E. Washington, D.C.

20002. Periodic issues entitled, *Hunger, Action* and *Update* reflecting U.S. Food Policy and legislation.

New Internationalist, New World Coalition, Room 209, 419 Boylston St., Boston, Mass. 02116. Published in Great Britian, an influential development periodical with penetrating analysis of issues.

Nutrition Action, monthly publication of Center for Science in the Public Interest, 1757 S St., N.W., Washington, D.C. 20009, Newsletter on nutrition, consumer and environmental problems.

One World, monthly magazine of the World Council of Churches, Communications Department of the WCC, 150 route de Ferne, P.O. Box 66, 1211 Geneva, 20, Switzerland.

A Shift in the Wind, published by the Hunger Project, P.O. Box 789, San Francisco, California 94101.

Sojourners, 1029 Vermont Avenue, N.W., Washington, D.C. 20005. Magazine of the Sojourners community with biblical perspective on justice, discipleship, and community.

Sustenance, the newsletter of the Action Center, formerly the Food Action Center, 1028 Connecticut Ave., N.W., #302, Washington, D.C. 20036

U.N. Development Forum, a monthly paper *free* from Center for Economic and Social Information, United Nations, New York, N.Y. 10017.

The Whale Report, published by the Center for Environmental Action, 2100 M. Street, N.W. Washington, D.C. 20037.

Christian Century, Scientific American, news magazines, deonominational mission oriented periodicals also carry information on the hunger/justice issue.

6. AUDIO-VISUAL RESOURCES

A World Hungry, a five-unit filmstrip series based on the work on C. Dean Freudenberger outlining facts and myths about hunger, the causes of hunger, international plans for justice, and personal responses in the areas of knowledge, life-style, church, and politics. Teleketics, 1229 South Santee Street, Los Angeles, Ca. 90015.

Beyond the Next Harvest, Film, color, 30 minutes. Mass-Media Ministries, 2116 N. Charles St., Baltimore, Md. 21280.

Bread for the World, Filmstrip, 20 minutes. Bread for the World, 207 East 16th Street, New York, NY 10003.

RESOURCES FOR STUDY AND ACTION

Sahel: Border of Hell, Film, 50 minutes. Post-Newsweek, New York, N.Y.

Hunger, Film, animated, color, 11 minutes. The Learning Corp. of America, 711 Fifth Avenue, New York, NY 10022.

Tilt, Film, color, animated, 19 minutes. Film Board of Canada. Distributed by CRM Education Films, Del Mar, Ca. 92014.

7. ORGANIZATIONS FIGHTING HUNGER

Alternatives, Box 20626, Greensboro, N.C., 27420.

Amnesty International, U.S.A. 2112 Broadway, New York, NY 10023.

Bread for the World, 207 East 16th Street, New York, NY 10003.

Center for Science in the Public Interest, 1757 S St. N.W. Washington, D.C. 20009.

Church World Service, 475 Riverside Drive, New York, NY 10027.

Hunger Project, The, P.O. Box 789, San Francisco, Ca. 94101.

Institute for Food and Development Policy, 2588. Mission, San Francisco, California 94110.

CROP, Box 968, Elkhard, IN 46514.

National Council of Churches Task Force on World Hunger, 475 Riverside Drive, New York, NY 10027.

Overseas Development Council, 1717 Massachusetts Ave., N.W. Washington, D.C. 20036.

Shakertown Pledge Group, c/o Friends Meeting House, W. 44th and York South, Minneapolis, Minn. 55410.

Washington Interreligious Staff Council/Hunger Task Force, 100 Maryland Ave., N.E. Washington, D.C.

WHEAT, 7820 Reading Road, Cincinnati, Ohio 45237.

World Council of Churches, 475 Riverside Drive, New York, NY 10027.

World Hunger Year (WHY), P.O. Box 1975, Garden City, N.Y 11530.

World Vision International, 912 W. Huntington Dr., Monrovia, Ca. 91016.

Worldwatch Institute, 1776 Massachusetts Ave., N.W. Washington, D.C. 20036.

INDEX OF SCRIPTURE

INDEX OF SCRIPTURE